FONTINA CASTELMAGNO CACIOCAVALLO TALEGGIO MONTE ENEBRO HUMB
NO-REGGIANO CHÈVRE NOIR MANOURI GOUDA FETA PROVOLONE STRACC
ROMAGER D'AFFINOIS MUNSTER MASCARPONE SB
BRIE CAMEMBERT ROBIOLA BOCCONCINI BURRATA FONTINA CASTELMAG
RUFFLE TREMOR FROMAGE BLANC CHEDDAR PARMIGIANO-REGGIANO CHÈV
MOZZARELLA PETIT BASQUE PRIMO SALE BEAUFORT FROMAGER D'AFFINO
ÉLICE DES CRÉMIERS GOAT TOMMINO GORGONZOLA BRIE CAMEMBERT RO
NTE ENEBRO HUMBOLDT FOG RICOTTA PECORINO TRUFFLE TREMOR FROMA
PROVOLONE STRACCHINO CASCIOTTA D'URBINO MOZZARELLA PETIT BASQ
ROQUEFORT RONCAL ROCCOLO GRUYÈRE LES DÉLICE DES CRÉMIERS GO
TINA CASTELMAGNO CACIOCAVALLO TALEGGIO MONTE ENEBRO HUMBOL
NO-REGGIANO CHÈVRE NOIR MANOURI GOUDA FETA PROVOLONE STRACCHI
ROMAGER D'AFFINOIS MUNSTER MASCARPONE SBRINZ ROQUEFORT RONCA
BRIE CAMEMBERT ROBIOLA BOCCONCINI BURRATA FONTINA CASTELMAGN
UFFLE TREMOR FROMAGE BLANC CHEDDAR PARMIGIANO-REGGIANO CHÈV
MOZZARELLA PETIT BASQUE PRIMO SALE BEAUFORT FROMAGER D'AFFINO
LICE DES CRÉMIERS GOAT TOMMINO GORGONZOLA BRIE CAMEMBERT ROB
NTE ENEBRO HUMBOLDT FOG RICOTTA PECORINO TRUFFLE TREMOR FROMA
PROVOLONE STRACCHINO CASCIOTTA D'URBINO MOZZARELLA PETIT BASQ

TOMMINO GORGONZOLA BRIE CAMEMBERT ROBIOLA BOCCONCINI BURRA
RICOTTA PECORINO TRUFFLE TREMOR FROMAGE BLANC CHEDDAR PARM
CIOTTA D'URBINO MOZZARELLA PETIT BASQUE PRIMO SALE BEAUFOR
CCOLO GRUYÈRE LES DÉLICE DES CRÉMIERS GOAT TOMMINO GORGONZ
CIOCAVALLO TALEGGIO MONTE ENEBRO HUMBOLDT FOG RICOTTA PECORIN
IR MANOURI GOUDA FETA PROVOLONE STRACCHINO CASCIOTTA D'URBIN
UNSTER MASCARPONE SBRINZ ROQUEFORT RONCAL ROCCOLO GRUYÈRE LE
A BOCCONCINI BURRATA FONTINA CASTELMAGNO CACIOCAVALLO TALEGGIO
ANC CHEDDAR PARMIGIANO-REGGIANO CHÈVRE NOIR MANOURI GOUDA F
IMO SALE BEAUFORT FROMAGER D'AFFINOIS MUNSTER MASCARPONE SE
OMMINO GORGONZOLA BRIE CAMEMBERT ROBIOLA BOCCONCINI BURRATA
G RICOTTA PECORINO TRUFFLE TREMOR FROMAGE BLANC CHEDDAR PARM
ASCIOTTA D'URBINO MOZZARELLA PETIT BASQUE PRIMO SALE BEAUFOR
CCOLO GRUYÈRE LES DÉLICE DES CRÉMIERS GOAT TOMMINO GORGONZ
CIOCAVALLO TALEGGIO MONTE ENEBRO HUMBOLDT FOG RICOTTA PECORIN
OIR MANOURI GOUDA FETA PROVOLONE STRACCHINO CASCIOTTA D'URBIN
UNSTER MASCARPONE SBRINZ ROQUEFORT RONCAL ROCCOLO GRUYÈRE L
A BOCCONCINI BURRATA FONTINA CASTELMAGNO CACIOCAVALLO TALEGGI
ANC CHEDDAR PARMIGIANO-REGGIANO CHÈVRE NOIR MANOURI GOUDA

THE CHEESEMONGER'S KITCHEN

THE

CHEESEMONGER'S

KITCHEN

CELEBRATING CHEESE IN 90 RECIPES

BY CHESTER HASTINGS

PHOTOGRAPHS BY
JOSEPH DE LEO

FOREWORD BY
PAUL ARATOW

CHRONICLE BOOKS
SAN FRANCISCO

Library of Congress Cataloging-in-Publication Data available.

ISBN 978-0-8118-7766-4

Manufactured in China

Designed by Vanessa Dina

Prop styling by Theo Vamvounakis

Food styling by Lori Powell

Typesetting by DC Type

Photographs on pages 6, 11, 21, 36, 50, 54, 59, 62, 77, 101, 120, 123,
132, 135, 139, 147, 167, 177, 190, 199, 205, 224 by Chester Hastings.

Joseph De Leo wishes to thank his crew for their talents and hard work,
his assistant Kazuhito Sakuma, Theo Vamvounakis, and Lori Powell.

10 9 8 7 6 5 4 3 2 1

Chronicle Books
680 Second Street
San Francisco, California 94107

WWW.CHRONICLEBOOKS.COM

for Susie

ACKNOWLEDGMENTS

First and foremost, this book would simply not have been possible to write without the overwhelming love and support of my beautiful wife, Susie. In the perfect storm of so many blessings all at once, she has stood by me and supported my efforts to do something a high-school dropout has little business doing—writing a book. I am eternally grateful to her for all she has been for me.

To Brian Kalliel, a longtime friend and demented master of wine: his ability to cut through the snobbery of the wine world is beyond refreshing. To Paul Aratow, thanks for being a wise and passionate soul whose obsession with the anthropological treasures of the culinary world rivals even my own. I would also like to thank Joan McNamara, my wife's mother, the grandmother to my two precious children, and the brilliant woman behind Joan's on Third. She is the reason I have been able to explore my passion for cheese for the last twelve years.

Thanks also to my agent, Margaret O'Connor. Many thanks to my loving sister-in-law, Carol McNamara, who is a constant source of support and enthusiasm, and to my best friend Dean McCreary, for his brilliant wit, which has kept me sane on more than one occasion.

My eternal gratitude goes to Carlo Middione, who started me on a discovery of food, art, music, and life that led me to places far and wide (*grazie, Capo, grazie!*). And finally to the artisans from all over the world who continue to hold out against the odds of politics and economic hardships to handcraft the world's finest cheeses.

TABLE
of
CONTENTS

FOREWORD

BY PAUL ARATOW

How wonderful to find a cookbook offering recipes that are truly new to the reader but also classic in their origins. And, as a dose of cognac to a bottle of Champagne, the revelations of discovery by Chester Hastings, a culinary Ulysses, are there for us to share with every recipe.

The evolution of culinary awareness in America has been revolutionary, with greater and greater emphasis on pure, fresh food prepared in a classic manner. New restaurants with an emphasis on what is the best of European cuisine combined with our contemporary appreciation for pure and fresh have proliferated, offering new menu choices for clients that are on the move toward a more sophisticated level of culinary awareness.

Chester Hastings is also on the move. From country boy to homeless, purple-Mohawked Berkeley street kid to top chef and successful restaurateur, Chester was on an exciting journey of profound discovery. Even from his youth, Chester had a dream of being a chef, and his opportunity came in the form of legendary chef Carlo Middione. Chester was hired off the street as a take-out food clerk in Chef Middione's iconic San Francisco Italian deli, Vivande Porta Via.

Soon, Chef Middione recognized Chester's passion and started classically training him. For Middione, that training began with books. For a year, Chester worked in the restaurant's basement storeroom under Middione's watchful guidance, studying Italian culture, literature, painting, architecture, agriculture, recipes, and cheese- and winemaking techniques throughout Italy, as well as the Italian language. Middione took him to the opera and museums.

Eventually Chester became second only to Middione in the kitchen. Then Middione sent him to Italy for fine tuning. Visiting with and cooking for aristocratic food dignitaries combined with visits to artisan bakeries, wineries, farms, and dairies, Chester returned to the states with a wealth of culinary knowledge and a mission.

This book is a precious amalgam of all that Chester's journey has taught him. Years of research and practice have gone into this book. In it you will see new ways of looking at cheese and benefit from the explanations of origin and fabrication that will allow us to taste cheese fully and deeply.

Most of us have experienced cheese as the viand that adorns the premeal cheeseboard, or, less often, the predessert platter, or topping on pizzas or hamburgers. In *The Cheesemonger's Kitchen*, we find a true integration of heat, cheese, and the magical chemistry of culinary expertise. In addition, our enjoyment of the dish is deepened by an understanding of the culture, the context, the humanity, that infuses the preparation and degustation. As a wonderful bonus, we have expert direction on the classic dilemma of what wine will be appropriate.

The Cheesemonger's Kitchen is a treasure of recipes that allows even the inexperienced cook to produce kitchen miracles. This book is down-to-earth in the best sense, not only offering us an appreciation of the sources and unique qualities of the cheeses suggested, but presenting that information in a clear and concise, even informal, manner, while still preserving the clarity necessary when following a new recipe.

"Look behind the document" is an expression in judicial language, but it serves us here very well. *The Cheesemonger's Kitchen* is more than a cookbook. Behind the document, the book is an experience waiting for the reader, a personal journey to new knowledge, even a new attitude toward food and cooking. A dish is not just something to be eaten—it is something to be experienced as a delicious cultural phenomenon, baptized with the essence of the fruit of the vine. Chester Hastings has offered us this marvelous possibility of a more profound culinary experience, and I, for one, am grateful for the opportunity to benefit from his amazing talent.

Chester has been instrumental in developing the elegant Cheesemonger's stand in the popular Los Angeles restaurant, Joan's on Third. It is his personal obsession to select the finest cheeses in order to share the glory of cheese and make the food of kings and peasants available to us all.

PAIRING WINE WITH CHEESE

BY BRIAN KALLIEL

Pairing wine with cheese is like riding a bike. It's all about finding balance.

The possible pairings of wine with cheese are countless. There are so many wines, so many cheeses—so many variables that go into a great pairing of wine and food in general—that it makes it difficult to nail down any hard and fast rules. This one factor generally leads me toward simple, well-balanced wines.

When I come across a combination of flavors, I often look for the main component that will counteract with wine and pair toward or against it. Sometimes it may be the cheese; sometimes it is some other ingredient. This is not to say that you shouldn't drink whatever you like with what you're eating, but if we're looking to elevate the flavors of both the wine and the food we eat with it, we must strive to put the components in balance with one another. For example, serving a mineral-rich Chardonnay with an earthy mushroom risotto is a nice balance of opposites, yet a high-acid Sauvignon Blanc pairs beautifully with a green salad dressed with an equally acidic vinaigrette. Many people love a fat, soft Sauternes with foie gras, although I love the contrasts of flavor and texture that a higher-tone Riesling offers with such a rich and fatty dish.

The diverse Old World flavors that Chester exposes us to are best matched with Mediterranean-style wines from all over the world, that have the verve to find balance in a wide range of flavors. There are some amazing wines that people are drinking every day, not all of which are the big showcases like DRC (Domaine de la Romanée-Conti) and GAJA. Overlooked varietals from France, Spain, and throughout Italy are not only great with food but can also be fantastic values. These are the wines I most often pair with food, the wines I share with my friends, and the wines that I am so happy to be sharing with you. If they seem esoteric at times, I can assure you that they are available at most wine merchants.

"The easiest way to grow as a person is to surround yourself with people smarter than you are." Whoever said that was right on the money, and no adage is truer for learning about wine. If you are really interested in knowing more about wine and how to pair it with food, then the best advice I can give you is to develop a relationship with your local wine merchant. Beyond supporting a small business in the community, you'll have a consistent source of knowledge and advice from people who make it their life's work to educate the public on the subject. Much like the relationship Chester encourages us to forge with local cheese-mongers, and far more effective than an Internet search, a regular conversation with a knowledgeable wine merchant about what you like and don't like can lead to some amazing discoveries.

Please note that where I suggest something like Cannonau (a gorgeous wine made from Grenache indigenous to Sardinia), your local wine merchant may offer a similar style Grenache or other comparable wine. This example is true of every wine suggested in this book. The profiles are what we are after more so than any specific wine.

PAIRING WINES WITH SPECIFIC MILK TYPES

GOAT'S MILK CHEESE

While there are many variations on goat cheese, from fresh and tangy to aged and sharp, they all tend to have that lemon acid in varying degrees. The prolific production of great goat cheeses from France's Loire Valley helps us see that Loire Valley wines are a great standard for pairing with goat cheeses in many forms. White grapes like Muscadet, Sauvignon Blanc, and Chenin Blanc produce crisp, mineral-driven wines, which counteract the dry acids of goat cheese and also brighten their gaminess. Balance. Therefore, these same grapes in other countries should pair equally well with these cheeses. In the case of goat cheese, pairing like with like, high-tone with high-tone works.

SHEEP'S MILK CHEESE

The earthiness in sheep's milk cheese is something to consider when looking for wine. By and large, sheep's milk cheese comes from Mediterranean climates. For me, medium-bodied, balanced whites and reds work best with these cheeses. The Sangiovese of central and southern Italy, Tempranillo and Garnacha of Spain, and the many reds in the south of France, from the Languedoc, Provence, and Rhone Valley regions, are also good candidates. Whites from dry Vernaccia di San Gimignano and sweet Vin Santo of Tuscany, all the way to the Chardonnay of Sicily, do well.

COW'S MILK CHEESE

While different goat cheeses share some basic qualities, the flavor profiles of sheep's and cow's milk cheeses run the gamut. When cheeses vary from soft, mild, runny, and pungent to hard, salty, and downright funky, here more than ever the idea of balance is key. Luckily, many of the wines that work with sheep's milk cheese also pair well with cow's milk cheeses. Light, fruit-driven wines ranging from Riesling and Vernaccia di San Gimignano to fruit-driven Chardonnay work for the semihard to hard cheeses. For soft and creamy cheeses, Champagne and Burgundy are nice. I prefer Chardonnay for funky soft cow's milk cheese. For red wines, stay away from tannins that compete with the high acidity found in the saltier hard cheeses. Dolcetto d'Alba and Bandol from Provence are good.

INTRODUCTION

THERE IS NO RIGHT OR WRONG
Really. It's the first thing I tell people who approach the cheese counter and, in an embarrassed tone, quickly admit that they don't know anything about cheese. Someone somewhere along the way made them feel that cheese, wine, food, or art, for that matter, is something about which one must know *everything* or might as well know nothing.

After assuring them that there truly is no right or wrong, I tell these people that what really matters is what they like. "I don't like blue cheese," some might offer. Okay. That's probably true, based on the few blue cheeses that they may have tasted. But what about the ones they haven't tried? In the end, they still may not love, or even like, blue cheese, but I encourage everyone to explore new foods at least once, especially cheeses, and to re-examine from time to time foods that they have sworn off since childhood.

When I was eleven years old, my mother and I were staying with her friend in Boston. On a drive from there up to Vermont, we stopped off at a roadside deli to pick up sandwiches. When my mother asked what I wanted, I replied, "Whatever you're having." What she was having was a massive hero sandwich, and it looked pretty good to me, crammed with cheese, bursting with salami, and dripping with oil and vinegar. But when I bit into the sandwich, I immediately spit it out. What was that foul, bitter taste? So went my first encounter with an anchovy.

I spent the better part of the next eight years avoiding anchovies like the plague until I was forced to eat them under the tutelage of my mentor, Carlo Middione. He had just returned from Sicily and had smuggled back a tin of anchovies packed in sea salt. Letting out a slight gasp of reverence at the sight of the "treasures" that had been carefully hand-layered into a vibrant baroque-style tin, he carefully rinsed a few of the creatures in cold water and, using his thumb, peeled open the bellies like an ancient book of illuminated manuscripts. With his fingertips, he gently removed the skeleton in one piece and laid out the anchovies on a plate. He then reached into his closely guarded knife box, took out a small vial of white truffle oil, and, with a single drop, gave each fillet an anointing. "Try one," he offered. And I did, forgoing the oath that I had made to my taste buds never to eat anchovies again. But what I tasted that day forever changed my feelings about anchovies. The flesh was meaty, almost sweet, and tasted clean, like the sea itself. There was no bitter aftertaste. The truffle oil added a perfume that did not mask or overpower the flavor but, rather, enhanced its earthy nuances in a perfect marriage.

Today I love anchovies. I owe countless moments of delight to that day when I gave them just one more shot. Clearly the quality of the salt-cured anchovies from Sicily was far superior to those squeezed out of a tube at that Vermont deli years ago, but I suspect it was also the context and gentle approach to a new flavor that allowed my mind and palate to stay open long enough for the newness of something to be explored.

I am constantly reminding people that it is okay that they do not know more about cheese. Most of us did not grow up with the variety of cheeses that are currently at our fingertips. We have a lot of catching up to do as we begin to incorporate them into our everyday diet. That bizarre cardboard-like powder atop overcooked spaghetti swimming in saccharin-sweet tomato sauce was the closest I came to Parmigiano-Reggiano until I was eighteen. Reading about cheese is great (and I am grateful that you're doing it now!), but nothing beats tasting cheese for yourself, especially when the cheese comes from a source that cares about where it comes from, how it is stored, and when it should be sold. I encourage you to find a cheese-monger in your neighborhood and create a relationship with him or her. Ask for samples, taste the cheese, think about it for a moment, and then ask questions about where it comes from, with what kind of milk it is made, and even how to serve and enjoy it. These are the basic questions that will begin your journey of discovery in the pantheon of great cheeses.

The proliferation of cheese shops and the expansive selection of cheese in larger chain markets is a growing opportunity for people who want to experience cheese on a daily basis as the Europeans have done for centuries. Unfortunately, many fine cheeses are sold in ways that intimidate the consumer or in pre-packed forms that are not only bad for the cheese but also hard on the wallet, forcing people to buy much more than they need. This often leads to spoilage, waste, and a wariness about buying cheese in the future. Buying cheese, or food in general, in smaller quantities when they are at their peak is the secret to the healthful, diverse, and delicious diets of places such as France and Italy.

ABOUT THE RECIPES

This book is a collection of some of my favorite ways to eat, serve, and enjoy cheese. It is by no means a comprehensive guide to the colossal world of cheese, but, rather, it is a sharing of my own experiences with what Clifton Fadiman called "milk's leap toward immortality."

Located in the list of ingredients of many Italian recipes is one of my favorite tools to cooking—the letters *Q.B.* This signifies a unit of measure that I encourage you to embrace in all of your cooking. The letters stand for *quanto basta*, literally meaning however much you think is needed is the correct amount. This is oh so true with cheese; many of the recipes presented here are merely my thoughts on amounts and types of cheese that have worked for me. "Quanto basta" does not apply to every ingredient, and certainly it applies less so in baking—including pastries—where the chemistry involved is more precise. The "quanto basta" idea is meant more as a reminder to experiment with what is available and what you enjoy eating and to follow your own tastes, as well as those of your friends and family. After all, it's unarguable that when it comes to following other people's recipes, all that really matters is that the dish becomes something you'll want to cook again.

A WORD ABOUT PARMIGIANO-REGGIANO

Parmigiano-Reggiano has become an indispensable cornerstone of the modern international diet, and as such, deserves special mention.

Benedictine and Cistercian monks first created Parmigiano-Reggiano in the thirteenth century. Thanks to very strict laws governing the production of "The King of Cheese," little has changed in the methods and ingredients used since its invention, and, therefore, the flavor of the cheese we are eating today is much like it must have been back then.

It is probably most thought of as a grating cheese, and it is indeed considered *the* grana, or "grain" cheese, because of its granular texture. But Parmigiano-Reggiano is very much a table cheese, and in Italy it is often served at the beginning of a meal with fresh figs, sweet melons, and cured salami. Parmigiano-Reggiano's relationship to the other crowned monarch of the region, Parma ham, goes beyond their delicious compatibility. Excess whey from the production of Parmigiano-Reggiano is fed to the sacred pigs whose hindquarters will become authentic prosciutto di Parma.

I always have a piece of Parmigiano-Reggiano on hand, though I generally keep small chunks that I am sure to use up before they lose their magic. When purchasing

Parmigiano-Reggiano, try to find large pieces of the whole wheel and ask the cheesemonger to cut from that piece. Avoid if you can Parmigiano-Reggiano that is pre-cut into smaller pieces and wrapped in plastic wrap/cling film, as the cheese starts to dry from the moment the wheel is opened and dies a little every day from that moment. I recommend not buying pre-grated Parmigiano-Reggiano, no matter how convenient it may seem. The flavors just aren't the same, and how much time and effort are we saving at the cost of such a loss of flavor?

FRESH GOAT CHEESE "PEARS" WITH PISTACHIO DUST / 27

FRESH GOAT CHEESE BUTTONS WITH
EDIBLE FLOWERS OR BRANDIED GOLDEN RAISINS / 28

GOAT CHEESE AND ROASTED GARLIC BEEHIVE / 29

TOMMINO CHEESE WITH SALSA VERDE AND ANCHOVIES / 33

TORTA DI GORGONZOLA / 34

BRIE WITH LIGURIAN OLIVE PASTE / 35

CHERRY TOMATO JAM FOR CHEESE / 37

CHEESE BOARDS

One great way to familiarize yourself with cheese and how to serve it is to make a cheese board. Here the cheeses can be savored, studied, and discussed in the privacy of your own home. At the end of the day, most great cheeses really should be eaten as they are in their purest forms. The recipes for cooking with the world's finest cheeses should be made with an appreciation for the cheeses as they come to us from the farm or *affineur* first.

TO START

Taste as much cheese as you can from where you purchase it and ask as much information as you can when doing so. Start a regular dialog with your local cheesemonger. Cheesemongers know a lot that you no doubt want to know as well. It is also a great idea to keep track of the basic facts about the cheeses you purchase. I go out of my way, no matter how busy I may be, to write down the name, type of milk, and country of origin of each cheese. This is the most basic information a cheesemonger can provide, and the most useful, for much like wine, what he or she thinks it tastes like doesn't really matter as much as what you think it tastes like. Having said that, knowing that the sheep's milk cheese is made by Benedictine monks who still receive a portion of the milk as a votive from local shepherds in the Pyrenees, or that the recipe for certain Pecorino from Romagna, Italy, was discovered when farmers hid their treasures in caves during the Saracen pirate raids, does add to the overall experience of fine cheese.

QUANTITY

When preparing a cheese board for a party, start with three to five cheeses. But, if cheese is being set out as an appetizer before a meal, you may want two—or even just one—very special selection. Too many cheeses on a board can start to overpower the palate and negate the unique and sometimes subtle qualities of each cheese. A general amount per person for a cheese board is roughly 1 to 2 oz/30 to 55 g per person of each cheese, though this depends greatly on what else is being served and where in the meal the cheese board is featured.

There is such a thing as too much cheese, and it is vital that you buy small amounts of what you will consume over the next few days, or even that evening, and then come back for more. I often cut people off, like a good bartender. I tell them they have enough cheese and ask them to come back when what they have is gone. It does no one any good to have beautiful cheese wasting away in the refrigerator. Being a cheesemonger means that I come in contact with, and there-fore consume, far more cheese on a daily basis than most. It is not a license to over-indulge, however. In fact, my love of good cheese prohibits overconsumption of it.

DESIGN

While entire cheese boards could be dedi-cated to a specific type of cheese, variety is certainly something to consider. Since everyone's palate is as different as his or her tastes, diversity is key for a cheeseboard.

Cheeses from the sheep's milk, cow's milk, and goat's milk categories are always nice to have represented, as well as a soft, semihard, and hard-textured cheese. Bring cheeses to room temperature before serving. I prefer to leave pieces of cheese whole and allow guests to take as little or as much as they like. Pre-slicing not only dries the cheese faster, but it also takes away from the simple and often rustic beauty of the cheese. In the case of aged cheeses like Parmigiano-Reggiano, some Pecorinos, and Goudas or Cheddars, walnut-size shards can be made with the tip of a cheese knife and piled high around the other cheeses.

Although I personally love to hover over a cheese board and talk about the various cheeses and where they come from, some simple handwritten signs with information about the cheese is a nice added touch. I am not one for heavily garnished food in general, opting more for the monochromatic feel of unadorned cheeses on a simple piece of wood or a white plate. It is a kind of statement: here is the cheese in all of its glory. When a bit of contrast is needed, a strategically placed lemon leaf or sprig of fresh herb is often enough.

ACCOMPANIMENTS

In selecting accompaniments to serve with cheese, consider not masking the flavor of the cheese but to contrast it in ways that further deepen the flavor profiles. Close your eyes, zero in on the main characteristic of the cheese, and then look for its contrast. Wildflower honey, cooked grape must, quince paste, and the famous mostardas of Italy can reveal the diverse flavors laying hidden just beneath the surface, but should never overpower the cheese in any way.

Here's a good rule of thumb: if the cheese is salty, it wants something sweet, and if it is sweet, it wants something salty. That may be overly simplified, but it works. Manchego from La Mancha, Spain, depending on the age, can be fairly salty; the typical accompaniment for this cheese is a thick paste made of cooked quince with sugar and a touch of lemon. The gentle sweetness balances out the salt and unlocks a deeper flavor of the precious raw sheep's milk that might otherwise be missed. When an unctuous cheese like raw–cow's milk Taleggio from Bergamo, Italy, or Stinking Bishop cheese from southwest England is met with a sweet and spicy mostarda of fruit cooked in sugar, water, and mustard oil, the superfunky perfume of the cheese is balanced by the sharp nasal-clearing powers of the mustard and the sweet syrup helps soften some of the slight bitterness at the end.

Fried Marcona almonds (known as the Queen of Almonds) from Andalusia, whole walnuts, toasted hazelnuts, dried apricots, and dried figs work wonders with cheese of all textures and flavor profiles. Agen prunes have been made since the thirteenth century and are unbelievable with fresh goat cheese or some of the deep blue cheeses like Valdeon, a mysterious cave-aged blue cheese of raw cow's and goat's milk wrapped in wine-soaked sycamore leaves.

Honey comes in a dizzying array of floral flavors. It can be used to great effect on any number of cheeses; chalky, earthy, and sweet milk Castelmagno from Cuneo, with its slight veins of blue, comes alive with a single stream of bitter chestnut honey. The deeply intense and goaty Monte Enebro wants the sweetness and airy floral aroma of a raspberry or citrus flower honey. Some cheeses have all the texture but may be a bit mild; mascarpone can be infused with white truffle honey to carry the treasured scent of truffles on a cloud of creamy cheese. And one of my favorite desserts on a summer day is fresh sheep's milk ricotta drizzled with honeysuckle honey and sprinkled with a pinch of ground espresso beans!

Of course, one of the best accompaniments to cheese can be the right wine. I agree with the great gastronomic writer Waverly Root when he says that wine cannot be divorced from food, that its very reason for being is to accompany food.

STORING
Cheese should be stored in wax/greaseproof paper in a separate drawer of the refrigerator if possible. Hard cheeses, like Parmigiano, can be wrapped well in aluminum foil, but no cheese should be stored in plastic wrap/cling film, as cheese is a living, breathing organism that needs some air.

Pistachios and fresh goat cheese is one of my favorite combinations. Use these "pears" to dress up a cheese board or dessert plate or even to serve with grilled lamb chops and a simple salad of arugula/rocket wildflowers, freshly squeezed lemon or grapefruit juice, and a peppery extra-virgin olive oil.

Pulse the pistachios in a spice grinder until powdery fine. Depending on the size of your grinder, it might be best to do this in a couple of batches. Pulsing the nuts will prevent them from turning into butter, which, while delicious, is not what we're going for here. If you do not own a spice grinder, some ambitious knife chopping will do just fine. Pass the ground pistachios through a fine-mesh sieve over a bowl to create an ultrasilky dust. Reserve the remaining pistachios from the sieve for cookies or cakes.

Divide the goat cheese into six golf ball–size pieces. Shape the balls into free-form pears, remembering that nature refuses to make any two alike, so you shouldn't try too hard either.

Roll the goat cheese "pears," one at a time, in the pistachio dust until well coated. Shake off any excess pistachio dust back into the bowl. After the cheese is coated, you can reshape it if needed, but the less it is handled, the brighter shade of green it will remain. Use the small herb leaves to make the "pear leaves."

The "pears" are best served the same day and can be made several hours before serving.

FRESH GOAT CHEESE "PEARS" WITH PISTACHIO DUST

MAKES 6 "PEARS"

½ cup/55 g shelled pistachios

12 oz/340 g fresh goat cheese

6 fresh herb leaves, such as marjoram or oregano

FRESH GOAT CHEESE BUTTONS WITH EDIBLE FLOWERS OR BRANDIED GOLDEN RAISINS

MAKES SIX 2-OZ/55-G BUTTONS

12 oz/340 g fresh goat cheese

6 edible flowers

¼ cup/150 g golden raisins/sultanas

2 tbsp brandy, Armagnac, or Calvados

Often piled up high on baskets lined with fresh rosemary or fragrant lavender, ultrafresh, locally made goat cheese adorned with a simple edible flower or fresh herb is one of my favorite sights at the farmers' market. These little buttons are great for tossing into a picnic basket with a crusty baguette and a crisp apple. I love Johnny-jump-ups for their diminutive size and magical look, but pansies, nasturtiums, and herb flowers are all lovely.

Other topping ideas include toasted pinhead oatmeal, fresh chives, sesame or poppy seeds, coarsely ground black peppercorns, Spanish smoked paprika, and chopped dried figs or apricots. Be creative.

Divide the goat cheese into six equal portions. Roll the cheese into smooth balls and then use your fingertips to shape the ball into a neat little square. Adorn the top of the cheese squares with an edible flower.

Soak the golden raisins/sultanas in the brandy for 30 minutes. Drain and gently pat dry with a clean kitchen towel. Arrange the golden raisins/sultanas in even rows atop the goat cheese squares and gently press them into the soft cheese. Reshape if needed.

Serve the same day for maximum freshness.

With its whimsical presentation and addictive flavor, this is a dish that deserves a platter all unto itself. Smaller beehives can be made for individual servings using small bowls or ramekins and are a fun way to dress up cheese boards, but the drama of a large beehive can't be beat.

The Goat Cheese and Roasted Garlic Beehive is an inspired creation of my mentor, Carlo Middione. His version calls for Bûcheron chèvre, but I have found that the fresh goat cheeses from upstate New York or Napa Valley, California, serve well for this dish and are far less costly.

Bennington Potters in Vermont makes a batter bowl with a shape that's perfect for creating a beehive appearance.

Preheat the oven to 400°F/200°C/gas 6.

Spread out the garlic on a baking sheet/tray and drizzle with the olive oil. Bake on the middle rack for 35 to 40 minutes, or until deep golden brown with burn spots here and there. Being careful not to burn your fingers, give the garlic heads a pinch. They should be very soft. Let cool to room temperature and then cut each head in half horizontally with a serrated bread knife.

Squeeze the roasted garlic pulp into a bowl, removing any garlic peels that may fall into the bowl. Mix the garlic pulp with a whisk until smooth. Save the peels to make a delicious roasted garlic stock for soup (see Roasted Garlic and Cauliflower Soup with Aged Cheddar, page 72).

cont'd

GOAT CHEESE AND ROASTED GARLIC BEEHIVE

SERVES 15 TO 20

5 lb/2.3 kg whole garlic heads, unpeeled

¼ cup/60 ml extra-virgin olive oil

2.2 lb/1 kg fresh goat cheese

Honey, warmed, for drizzling

Crostini, crackers, or crusty bread, for serving

Line a 1-qt/960-ml bowl with cheesecloth/muslin with plenty of overhang. Bring the goat cheese to room temperature.

Using clean and slightly damp hands, press a small amount of the cheese into the cloth-lined bowl. It should be a layer about 1 in/2.5 cm thick. This will be the top of the beehive. Add enough garlic puree to make a layer about 1 in/2.5 cm thick; repeat with the goat cheese, forming it into a disc 1 in/2.5 cm thick and of the same circumference of the mold. Continue with the alternating layers of goat cheese and garlic, ending with the cheese. Cover with the overhanging cheesecloth/muslin and refrigerate overnight.

An hour or so before serving, peel back the cheesecloth/muslin. Place a cake stand upside down on the bowl and then invert the two together. Remove the bowl and peel off the cheesecloth/muslin to reveal the beehive. Any cracks in the goat cheese can be smoothed with a wet finger or spatula. Drizzle the beehive with honey to complete the theme and balance the aromatic garlic.

Serve with crostini, crackers, or plenty of crusty bread.

Salsa verde is a traditional sauce for serving with anchovies as an antipasto. It is also a wonderful accompaniment to grilled/barbecued meat, fish, and chicken, as well as a fantastic dipping sauce for homemade bread! The marriage of fresh goat's milk cheese with this sauce is one made in heaven.

Anchovies have a long and practical history in the cooking of Piedmont, Italy. It is said that when salt taxes were imposed within the landlocked region, the anchovy, which was packed and cured in salt, could be used to replace the precious mineral in cooking as a way to save money.

TO PREPARE THE SALSA VERDE: Boil the garlic in a small pan of water for 2 minutes, to mellow out the flavors. Using a mortar and pestle (or a food processor if you must), grind together the garlic, parsley, basil, egg yolk, chile, and lemon juice to create a dark green paste, as smooth or as coarse as you please. Slowly add the olive oil. The salsa verde should be used the day of preparation.

TO ASSEMBLE THE DISH: If using salt-cured anchovies, rinse them under cold water to remove the salt. Using your thumb, pry open the belly of each fish and carefully open like a book. Take hold of the skeleton bones on the opposite end from the tail and gently pull downward, removing them in one piece. Pat the flesh dry on paper towels. (Anchovies can be dressed with olive oil and kept like this for several days in the refrigerator, though I prefer to clean them as needed.)

Place the cheese on a platter or individual plates. Top each button with a dollop of the salsa verde and garnish with an anchovy fillet before serving.

TOMMINO CHEESE WITH SALSA VERDE AND ANCHOVIES

SERVES 5 TO 10

FOR THE SALSA VERDE
2 garlic cloves, peeled

½ bunch fresh flat-leaf parsley

¼ cup/8 g fresh basil leaves

1 hard-boiled egg yolk

1 small hot chile, or pinch of dried chili flakes

Juice of 1 small lemon

⅔ cup/165 ml extra-virgin olive oil

FOR ASSEMBLING THE DISH
10 anchovies (either salt-cured from Sicily, or very best-quality tinned in olive oil), for garnish

10 small buttons of Tommino or other fresh goat cheese, roughly 2 oz/55 g each

TORTA DI GORGONZOLA

SERVES 15 TO 20

1 lb/455 g mascarpone cheese

2.25 lb/1 kg Gorgonzola dolce latte cheese (in one piece)

½ cup/115 g pine nuts, toasted

Oat crackers or focaccia, for serving (optional)

I first experienced this heavenly concoction at Peck, the stunning food emporium in Milan. Slabs of "sweet milk" Gorgonzola (a rich and creamy cow's milk blue from Italy's Lombardy region) layered with mascarpone (a tangy triple-cream cheese made from crème fraîche) are topped with toasted walnuts or pine nuts. It is a wonderful treat at holiday gatherings, where its dramatic presentation can be fully appreciated. Let guests serve themselves, perhaps with fresh figs when they are in season, a bowl of warm honey on the side, or even a pear mostarda.

The torta can be made in smaller sizes, but I like to make this big version, as the leftovers make for a simple yet decadent pasta sauce. Simply bring 2 oz/55 g of Torta di Gorgonzola per person to room temperature and toss with 5 oz/140 g fresh pasta per person straight from the boiling water. Add a handful of grated Parmigiano and loads of freshly cracked black pepper to finish.

Mix the mascarpone with a spoon until creamy. Cut the Gorgonzola into four equal slices horizontally. If it is very ripe, it may be a bit messy to work with, although the flavor will be that much better. Spread a quarter of the mascarpone over the first slice of Gorgonzola as if you were icing an old-fashioned chocolate cake. Place the second layer of Gorgonzola atop the mascarpone and continue, ending with the mascarpone on top. Resist the temptation to spread the mascarpone smooth, as the frosting-like waves give this torta its irresistible look. Top with the pine nuts and serve with oat crackers, if desired.

Here a wheel of Brie is sliced in half horizontally; spread with a glistening paste of Ligurian olives, fried garlic, and capers; and then reassembled for the cheese board.

True raw-milk Brie is a sad casualty of laws prohibiting many soft raw-milk cheeses into the United States. As a result, "brie" is now made all over the world, sometimes with surprisingly good qualities and other times with a less-stellar outcome. For this recipe a wheel that is too ripe and runny will be difficult to cut in half. Another cheese that lends itself well to a layer of olive paste is the little button of fresh goat's milk, called *Picandou*, from the Perigord region of France.

This recipe for Ligurian Olive Paste yields considerably more than you will need for the Brie, but it will keep for weeks in a clean glass jar in the refrigerator. It is also fantastic tossed with a bit of cooked pasta (either hot or cold), with a healthy pinch of chili, and perhaps a few anchovies.

TO PREPARE THE LIGURIAN OLIVE PASTE: Place the olives and capers in the bowl of a food processor fitted with the blade attachment. In a small frying pan, cook the garlic with the olive oil over medium heat, turning over the garlic as one side becomes lightly golden. (Be careful not to burn them.) When both sides of the garlic are cooked, pour the oil and garlic over the olives and capers. Add the lemon zest and pulse until smooth, scraping down the sides of the bowl once or twice.

TO PREPARE THE BRIE: Cut the Brie in half lengthwise using a sharp knife or a long piece of kitchen string wrapped around the edges and then pulled toward you. Spread 2 tbsp of the olive paste evenly on the bottom piece of Brie and then replace the top piece. Garnish with olive leaves and serve.

BRIE WITH LIGURIAN OLIVE PASTE

MAKES 1 CUP PASTE; SERVES 4 TO 6

FOR THE LIGURIAN OLIVE PASTE
½ lb/225 g *taggiasca*, niçoise or other black olives, pitted

2 tbsp capers, drained

2 garlic cloves, peeled

¼ cup/60 ml extra-virgin olive oil

Zest of 1 lemon

FOR THE BRIE
1 small wheel Brie, about 9 oz/255 g

Fresh olive leaves or herbs, for garnish

This is a sweet condiment for cheese with all the earthy perfume of a garden tomato. If the idea sounds a bit unusual, it may help to remember that tomatoes are fruit. Please try—just try—to grow your own tomatoes, especially cherry tomatoes, which can be grown on a windowsill with little fuss. The rewards of homegrown tomatoes are simply too great not to give growing them a go.

For this jam, I actually prefer to make small batches to consume within a week or two, which gives me a great reason to have a cheese-centric get together with loads of friends. Remember: this is an accompaniment to the cheese and should be used sparingly.

This jam works gloriously on fresh creamy goat cheese like Tomme de Ma Grande-mère from the Loire Valley in France, fresh Robiola from Northern Italy, Cana de Cabra from Spain, and especially aged pecorino. One of my favorite pecorinos is the wonderful Staginonato Foglie di Noci, a sheep's milk cheese from Pienza, Italy, which is wrapped in walnut leaves before being placed in terra-cotta pots for six months!

CHERRY TOMATO JAM FOR CHEESE

MAKES 1½ CUPS/360 ML

2 cups/340 g cherry or grape tomatoes

¾ cup/150 g sugar

3 tbsp freshly squeezed lemon juice

Zest of 1 lemon

½ tsp fresh rosemary, finely chopped

Heat the oven to 350°F/180°C/gas 4.

Cut the tomatoes in half and place on a baking sheet/ tray lined with aluminum foil. Bake for about 15 minutes to loosen the skins. Remove the tomatoes from the oven and let cool slightly before carefully peeling away the skins.

Place the tomatoes and the sugar over medium heat and gently melt the sugar. Bring to a boil and cook, boiling rapidly, for 5 to 7 minutes, or until thick and syrupy. Remove from the heat and stir in the lemon juice, lemon zest, and rosemary.

Transfer to a clean, sterilized jar and seal well. The jam can be kept refrigerated for 2 weeks, though I doubt it will make it that long!

BAKED APPLES WITH CAMEMBERT AND
GOOSE-FAT-FRIED DIPPING POTATOES / 41

GRILLED CAMEMBERT / 44

BRESAOLA WITH ROBIOLA DI ROCCAVERANO
AND WHITE TRUFFLE OIL / 45

BROILED BOCCONCINI DI PURA CAPRA
WRAPPED IN SPECK / 47

BURRATA WITH ASPARAGUS, PINE NUTS,
AND GOLDEN RAISINS / 49

FONTINA FONDUTA WITH
WHITE TRUFFLE BUTTER / 51

CASTELMAGNO AND HAZELNUT FONDUTA / 52

FRIED CACIOCAVALLO,
THE POOR MAN'S STEAK / 53

TALEGGIO FRIED IN
CORNMEAL AND GRAPPA BATTER / 55

FRIED MONTE ENEBRO WITH RASPBERRY BLOSSOM HONEY / 56

PUFF PASTRY PILLOWS WITH HUMBOLDT FOG,
RED ONION, AND WILD HONEY–SYRAH SYRUP / 57

GOUGÈRES / 60

SAVORY LEMON, RICOTTA, AND PECORINO FRITTERS / 61

ROBIOLA VERDE / 63

TWICE-BAKED TRUFFLE TREMOR SOUFFLÉ / 64

APPETIZERS

The moment guests begin arriving for dinner is a moment of love and hate. On the one hand, you are excited to spend time with friends and family who have gathered in your home to break bread (and "ooh" and "aah" over the delicious dinner you have been creating all day). On the other hand, they're here, and you can't spend time with them because you're still creating that same delicious dinner for them to all "ooh" and "aah" over!

Passed hors d'oeuvres and trays of prepared delicacies not only buy that extra bit of time you inevitably need in the final moments, but they can even be an enticing promise of the dinner to come.

Most modern families eat more or less family style, and many of the dishes in this chapter are right at home as side dishes to the main meal. The magic of having just one starter course to kick things off is really nice, however, and this dish often acts as the ritual bell to invoke the spirit of what having company really means. A gathering of people around the sacred act of eating is no small thing, and I try to remember this even as I wish there had been just a bit more traffic that evening.

WINE NOTE

Generally speaking, wines poured at the opening of the dinner, especially reds, should be lighter than wines served later in the meal. We don't start with the entrée, so why start with an entrée-weight wine?

Appetizers encourage hunger, and lighter, more acidic aperitif wines are meant to do the same. Champagne, Prosescco, Cava, Chenin Blanc, Arneis, and Sauvignon Blanc—all of these are white wines—whet the appetite with their properties of acidity, lower sugar, and minerality.

On the other hand, heavy wines, with their high sugar and alcohol contents, can have the same effect as food—they curb the appetite. If you desire a red wine to serve with your appetizers, Gamay, Chinon, Dolcetto, young Sangiovese, and Rioja are all great wines with which to begin.

Maybe it was just because it was the last day of an unforgettable honeymoon that had taken us through the foie gras–infested fairytale of the Dordogne, into the sun-drenched antique markets of Provence, and over the Auvergne hills filled with farmsteads selling Cantal cheese, culminating in my very first time in Paris. Or maybe it was the perfect simplicity of crisp green apples and real raw-milk Camembert served together in a new and surprising way. Whatever it was, our last meal before returning home was somehow the most memorable. Exhausted from the June heat, we literally stumbled into a sidewalk café, sat down, and ordered from the small chalkboard at our table.

As if the decadence of ooey gooey melted Camembert inside a hollowed-out apple weren't enough, we were served potatoes fried to a golden crisp in goose fat for dipping in the cheese! It was all washed down with a crisp, dry white wine of unknown local variety.

This is great as an afternoon lunch with a simple green salad or as a first course to a summer meal. Do not forget to eat the apple when all the cheese is gone!

cont'd

BAKED APPLES WITH CAMEMBERT AND GOOSE-FAT-FRIED DIPPING POTATOES

SERVES 4

BAKED APPLES WITH CAMEMBERT

4 Granny Smith or other tart green apples

One 8 oz/225 g wheel ripe Camembert cheese

4 tbsp/55 g butter, at room temperature

¼ cup/60 ml Calvados or dry white wine

Preheat the oven to 375°F/190°C/gas 5.

Cut off the tops of the apples, about ¼ in/6 mm from the top, and set the lids aside. Core the apples. Using a sharp knife, gently score them vertically in four places just enough to cut through the skin, to prevent the apples from bursting during cooking.

Tear the Camembert into small pieces and divide among the apples, filling each cavity. Replace the lids, slightly askew, and rub the apples with the butter. Place the stuffed apples in an 8-by-10-in/20-by-30.5-cm baking dish or on a baking sheet/tray lined with parchment/baking paper, leaving plenty of space between them. Sprinkle with the Calvados and place on the middle rack of the oven.

Bake for 35 to 40 minutes, or until the apples are tender but not falling apart and the cheese has completely melted.

GOOSE-FAT-FRIED DIPPING POTATOES

2 cups/480 ml rendered goose or duck fat*

2 russet potatoes

Sea salt

*Rendered duck fat is quite simple to make (see facing page), although it can be found in many specialty food stores, either domestic brands such as D'Artagnan or even Rougie from the Perigord region, France.

In a deep saucepan, gently melt the goose fat and heat to 120°F/48°C. (Use a standard kitchen thermometer to check the temperature.) Meanwhile, peel the potatoes, slice into ⅛-in/3-mm rounds, and place in a bowl of cold water to keep the slices from oxidizing. When the fat is hot, drain the potato slices, pat them dry with a kitchen towel, and then cook in small batches for 10 to 12 minutes, or until fork tender. Remove from the fat and drain on heavy paper. (This is a great way to reuse paper grocery bags!)

When all the potatoes are cooked, increase the heat on the fat to 160°F/70°C. Add the cooked potato slices, again in small batches so as not to cool the fat, and fry for about 2 minutes, or until golden brown and crispy. Remove to a sheet of paper and season with plenty of sea salt.

Serve the apples hot, with plenty of dipping potatoes.

WHITE WINE: Champagne, Prosecco, Vernaccia di San Gimignano
OTHER: sparkling cider from Normandy, Calvados

RENDERED DUCK FAT

**Skin and fat from 1 whole duck
(ask your butcher to provide)**

½ cup/120 ml cold water

Cut the skin and fat into 1-in/2.5-cm cubes and place in a heavy-bottomed pot.
Add the water and simmer over medium heat until the water evaporates and the
skin pieces are crisp and have released all their fat, about 1 hour.

Strain the clear golden fat through a sieve. Rendered duck fat can be
kept in a sealed container in the refrigerator for several days, or in the freezer
for several months. The crispy skin pieces can be sprinkled with salt and enjoyed
in secret!

GRILLED CAMEMBERT

SERVES 2 TO 4

**One 8 oz/225 g wheel ripe
Camembert cheese, in its box**

Sea salt

1 baguette, toasted, for serving

Heating Camembert over hot flames, wood or charcoal if possible, brings the cheese to a texture and temperature that maximizes the flavors.

Unfortunately for many of us, due to antiquated concepts of health and paranoid lawmakers, true Camembert made of raw cow's milk, like Brie, is but a dream of a better time to come. Still, there are some very good pasteurized Camemberts sold outside of France, though they may lack the complexity of flavor that the raw-milk versions have. All the more reason why recipes like this make sense. Granted, if you get your hands on the real deal (don't ask; don't tell), this preparation will be so much the better.

Preheat a gas grill/barbecue to medium-high heat or build a medium-hot fire in a charcoal grill/barbecue.

Take the cheese out of its box and unwrap. Carefully slice the rind off the top and then return the cheese to its box, cut-side up, and sprinkle with a pinch of sea salt.

Place the box directly on the hot grill/barbecue, cut-side up, and cook for 10 to 12 minutes, or until the cheese is warm and melted. The box may burn a bit, which is not only fine but adds a dramatic appearance that I find pleasing.

Remove from the grill/barbecue and serve hot with pieces of toasted baguette.

· ·

WHITE WINE: Chardonnay
RED WINE: Beaujolais, Gamay, Valle d'Aosta

Robiola is a family of creamy fresh cheeses that are produced across northern Italy, from Cuneo and Asti in Piedmont all the way to Lombardy, varying widely depending on where it is made. All are worth experiencing, though it is the Robiola di Roccaverano from outside Cuneo that I find is one of the very best.

Fresh cheese making in this area dates back to Celtic times, and even Pliny the Elder extolled its great virtues. While tradition and even law (Robiola di Roccaverano is the only Robiola cheese with a *Denominazione de Origine Protetta*, or DOP, status, ensuring that the ingredients and techniques from ancient times are maintained in the modern production) maintain that Robiola di Roccaverano must be made with a minimum of 50 percent goat's milk—the remaining milk coming from either sheep or cow—there is a rare version of the cheese made of 100 percent pure goat's milk, Robiola di Roccaverano Pura Capra. For your sake and the sake of your cheese-loving soul, I implore you to seek out the Pura Capra version.

Bresaola is a mild, air-cured beef tenderloin from Piedmont, although there are some amazing versions from Uruguay to be had as well.

Lay the slices of bresaola out on a work surface and divide the Robiola evenly among them, placing the cheese on one end of the slice. Starting with the cheese side, roll the bresaola over on itself to form a roll, leaving a small "tongue" sticking out at the end. Anoint each roll with a single drop of truffle oil, no more, as the flavor will overpower the others at work. Arrange the rolls on a platter with a few sprigs of fresh oregano and serve immediately with breadsticks.

RED WINE: Valtellina, Nebbiolo-based wines, Bandol, Rioja

BRESAOLA WITH ROBIOLA DI ROCCAVERANO AND WHITE TRUFFLE OIL

MAKES 16 PIECES

16 paper-thin slices of bresaola

6 oz/170 g Robiola di Roccaverano Pura Capra or other fresh Robiola cheese

A small amount of certified organic white truffle oil*

Fresh oregano sprigs, for garnish

Breadsticks or crostini, for serving

*Certified organic truffle oil is made without chemical additives, which unfortunately cannot be said of the glut of truffle oils on the market. The price of a better-quality infused truffle oil should not be too intimidating, as it is still a far cry from spending the money that fresh truffles demand.

Bocconcini di Pura Capra are soft little pillows of bloom-rind goat's milk cheese made in Piedmont, Italy, at the Caseificio Alta Langa. They are delicate, gooey, and creamy with a rich but not overly goaty flavor. They are perfect picnic cheeses as they are, but if I am near an open flame or a broiler/grill when I have them, I cannot resist wrapping them in a piece of prosciutto, pancetta, or speck and giving them a quick blast of heat. The word *bocconcini* literally translates to "little mouthfuls," and while the makers of the cheese were no doubt referring to the diminutive size of these cheeses, this recipe always has me greedily trying to get the whole thing in my mouth at once. The perfect combination and simple preparation make me smile every time.

Bocconcini di Pura Capra is becoming more and more widely available at cheese shops and better quality grocers, though Marcellin and even Andante Dairy's Accapella are also good options.

Speck is a gently smoked ham from the Tyrol on the Italian-Austrian border. In addition to a delicate smoky flavor, traditional speck has the perfume of juniper berries, which are used in the speck-curing process.

Preheat the oven to broil/grill.
Remove the paper from the cheese and wrap the meat around them like a ribbon around a present. Place on a baking sheet/tray and broil/grill for 3 to 5 minutes, until the meat is crisp and the cheese has begun to bubble. Remove and serve immediately with crusty bread and perhaps some fresh arugula/rocket, if desired.

WHITE WINE: Roero Arneis, Chardonnay
RED WINE: Chinon, Barolo

BROILED BOCCONCINI DI PURA CAPRA WRAPPED IN SPECK

SERVES 4

4 disks Bocconcini di Pura Capra cheese

4 paper-thin slices speck, prosciutto, or pancetta

Crusty bread, for serving

Arugula/rocket, for serving (optional)

The distinctly Sicilian combination of pine nuts, raisins, and bread crumbs is quickly becoming a classic around the world, used in everything from light pastas with fried sardines and fennel to fillings for swordfish or beefsteak rolls. Here, these flavors are combined in a lovely, light springtime presentation of early April asparagus and fresh Burrata cheese. Saffron, used judiciously, adds a lovely perfume and an elegant effect if the threads are left whole. A thin slice of prosciutto di Parma would be a welcome addition to this dish, simply served alongside or draped over the top to hide the jewel of a salad underneath.

Cut the woody ends off the asparagus and discard. Blanch the asparagus spears in plenty of salted boiling water for 2 to 4 minutes, or until tender and just starting to give when pinched where the tip begins. Do not overcook! Shock the asparagus quickly in a bowl of ice water, drain, and then dry thoroughly with paper towels. Cut the asparagus on the angle into pieces resembling penne pasta.

Soak the golden raisins/sultanas in warm water for 5 minutes to rehydrate and then drain and pat dry with a kitchen towel. In a large bowl, combine the asparagus with the pine nuts, raisins/sultanas, saffron, and 2 tbsp of the olive oil. Season with salt and freshly cracked black pepper.

Heat ¼ cup/60 ml of the remaining olive oil over a medium heat and add the bread crumbs. Shake the pan vigorously, frying the bread crumbs for about 1 minute, or until light golden and crisp. Remove from the heat and set aside.

Cut the Burrata balls in half and place on individual plates "skin-side" down. Divide the asparagus mixture among the Burrata pieces and sprinkle the fried bread crumbs over the top.

Drizzle with the remaining olive oil and serve cold or at room temperature.

WHITE WINE: Vermentino di Gallura, Grüner Veltliner

BURRATA WITH ASPARAGUS, PINE NUTS, AND GOLDEN RAISINS

SERVES 4

9 oz/255 g asparagus

2 tbsp golden raisins/sultanas

2 tbsp toasted pine nuts

6 threads of saffron

½ cup/120 ml best-quality extra-virgin olive oil

Salt and freshly cracked black pepper

¼ cup/30 g bread crumbs

2 balls fresh Burrata cheese, roughly 6 oz/170 g each

The basic technique of slowly melting a single cheese, such as the Italian Fontina Valle d'Aosta, with the help of whole milk, rich egg yolks, and the best-quality butter can also be applied to several different cheeses blended to your own taste.

When shopping for fontina, look for real Fontina Valle d'Aosta, which is marked with the official "Fontina Zona di Produzione Regione Autonoma, Valle d'Aosta, DOP." The unbelievable quality of the raw milk, the mastered traditional techniques employed, and the singularly sweet flavors from the spruce-wood shelves on which the cheese wheels are aged cannot be mimicked or replicated anywhere else in the world.

If you have access to fresh white truffles, thinly slice them over the top of this *fonduta*. More than likely, you'll need a drizzle of truffle oil or—as I prefer—a beautiful farm butter from the Poitou-Charentes region of France studded with fresh white truffles as shown in the photograph.

Place the fontina and half of the milk in a double boiler or a large bowl set over a pot of boiling water. When the cheese begins to melt, add a few grindings of black pepper. Stir gently with a wooden spoon for 12 to 15 minutes, or until the cheese is completely melted. Add the egg yolks and the butter and stir to combine. Meanwhile, gently warm the remaining cup of milk in another saucepan. Slowly add the warm milk to the fonduta and stir well until smooth.

Pour into a large fondue pot or divide among individual fondue pots and serve hot with skewers of bread cubes.

FONTINA FONDUTA WITH WHITE TRUFFLE BUTTER

SERVES 8

½ lb/225 g Fontina Valle d'Aosta cheese, cut into 1-in/2.5-cm cubes

2 cups/480 ml whole milk

Freshly cracked black pepper

4 egg yolks, beaten

8 oz/225 g white truffle butter, at room temperature

Bread, cubed, for dipping

WHITE WINE: bright, earthy wines such as Vinho Verde, Rousanne, Côte du Rhone Blanc, American Grenache Blanc
RED WINE: Pinot Noir (especially soft styles from Oregon), Sangiovese
OTHER: Rosé

CASTELMAGNO AND HAZELNUT FONDUTA

SERVES 4

4 oz/115 g Castelmagno cheese, finely grated

½ cup/120 ml heavy/double cream

1 egg yolk

Hazelnuts, toasted and crushed

Crusty bread, for dipping

Pears, for dipping

Another fonduta I have to mention is an even simpler affair, made with the ancient cheese Castelmagno. A chalky, intense, dry cow's milk cheese from Cuneo, Italy, that has been in production since the early eleventh century, Castelmagno is supposedly named after San Magno, a Roman soldier who was killed in the mountains near Cuneo and became a local martyr. Often crumbled over hot risotto or delicate gnocchi, Castelmagno's faint hint of blue is glorious when fully melted into a fonduta.

Combine the cheese and cream in a double boiler or a bowl placed over a pot of boiling water. Stir gently with a wooden spoon until the cheese is melted and well amalgamated with the cream, about 10 minutes. At this point, stir a bit more vigorously, for about 2 minutes, to incorporate a bit of air. Remove from the heat and quickly add the egg yolk, stirring rapidly to combine. The fonduta is now ready. Pour it into a fondue pot. For a bit of texture, toss a handful of crushed toasted hazelnuts over the top before serving with chunks of crusty bread or skewers of ripe pears.

WHITE WINE: Gavi di Gavi, Orvieto, Chardonnay
RED WINE: wines from truffle country like Nebbiolo, Barbera d'Alba, Dolcetto, and Sagrantino

In Sicily, where meat has historically been a rare luxury for the poor, this fried cheese was invented to mimic the pan-fried steaks of the wealthy silversmith.

Caciocavallo literally translates as "horse cheese," so-named because two balls are often tied together by rope and thrown over a mule's neck like saddlebags to bring the cheeses to market. It is a wonderfully sharp and salty provolone-style cheese that lends itself well as a main ingredient when cooking with pasta, as filling for meats, or, in this case, as the meal itself!

Heat the olive oil in a large frying pan over low heat. Add the garlic, fry until golden brown on both sides, about 1 minute per side, and then discard. Turn up the heat to medium-high and add the slices of cheese. Fry the cheese for 2 or 3 minutes on each side, until the edges begin to gild. Splash the vinegar over the cheese in the pan and sprinkle in the oregano and pepper. Turn up the heat to high and cook for 1 minute more. Carefully place the cheese slices on hot plates and serve immediately with lots of crusty bread.

WHITE WINE: Sicilian Chardonnay
RED WINE: Nero d'Avola, Cerasuolo

FRIED CACIOCAVALLO, THE POOR MAN'S STEAK

SERVES 4

¼ cup/60 ml extra-virgin olive oil

3 garlic cloves, peeled

4 slices Caciocavallo cheese, ¾ in/2 cm thick

2 tbsp best-quality red wine vinegar

2 tbsp fresh oregano, or 1 tbsp dried

Freshly cracked black pepper

Crusty Italian bread or baguette, for serving

Taleggio is from a family of cheeses known as *stracchino*, which means "tired." The morning milking is skipped, allowing the cows to graze all day long with that extra milk literally churning in their stomachs, raising the butterfat to an all time high and resulting in very rich milk that evening. Taleggio is very creamy, sweet, tangy, and slightly funky in that wonderful barnyard way. There are several raw-milk varieties available, and I encourage you to seek them out at your local cheese shop. This is fantastic served with a pear or apricot mostarda.

Cut the Taleggio into eight slices, about ¼ in/6 mm thick, and keep chilled in the refrigerator until ready to fry.

In a medium bowl, make a batter by whisking together the flour, cornmeal, grappa, and egg yolk until smooth. Season with salt and pepper.

Meanwhile, in a deep fryer or heavy saucepan, heat the oil to 360°F/185°C. Dredge the Taleggio slices in the batter, shaking off any excess, and fry for about 2 minutes, or until golden brown. Drain on paper towels or paper bags and serve immediately.

WHITE WINE: Chardonnay, Grüner Veltliner
RED WINE: sparkling reds low in alcohol like Lambrusco or Bugey

TALEGGIO FRIED IN CORNMEAL AND GRAPPA BATTER

SERVES 6

1 lb/455 g Taleggio cheese, rind removed

½ cup/60 g all-purpose/plain flour

½ cup/70 g cornmeal

½ cup/120 ml grappa or dry white wine

1 egg yolk

Salt and freshly ground black pepper

2 cups/480 ml pure olive oil for frying

FRIED MONTE ENEBRO WITH RASPBERRY BLOSSOM HONEY

SERVES 4

½ cup/120 ml extra-virgin olive oil

11 oz/310 g Monte Enebro cheese, cut into 4 equal slices

½ cup/60 g all-purpose/plain flour

2 eggs, beaten

6 tbsp/90 ml raspberry blossom honey, warmed

Monte Enebro was invented by Rafael Baez in Avila, Spain, roughly fifteen years ago. He still makes this cheese by hand with his daughter, Paloma, from local goat's milk inoculated with the same strain of mold used in Roquefort cheese. The cheese is formed into logs and then cured in caves. I have always adored eating this cheese with fresh peaches or dried Agen prunes, but then I read about what inventive chef José Pizarro in London was doing with it: deep-frying slabs of the stuff and drizzling citrus flower honey over it! Yes, please!

The following is an interpretation of his now-famous dish, and I have discovered that different honey varieties can actually do very different things to this dish. I encourage you to explore as I have.

Heat the olive oil in a medium frying pan over medium-high heat until hot but not smoking. Dredge the cheese slices in the flour, shaking off any excess, and then in the beaten eggs. Carefully slide the slices into the hot oil, moving in a direction away from you to prevent any backsplash of hot oil. Fry the cheese for 15 to 30 seconds, until a golden crust forms, and then turn over the slices. Spoon hot oil onto the top sides of the cheese as it cooks for another 15 to 30 seconds, or until the second sides are golden and crisp.

Remove the cheese from the pan, drain on paper bags, and transfer the slices to warm plates. Drizzle the honey over the fried cheese and serve immediately.

WHITE WINE: Savennières, Châteauneuf-du-Pape Blanc

In Humboldt County, California, Mary Keehn began raising Alpine goats simply because there were no sources of healthful goat's milk for her children. She discovered a natural talent for selectively breeding goats and soon found herself with an unexpected consequence; surplus milk from more than fifty goats! Mary took to her kitchen with an incredible sense of can-do, as well as a knack for creating delicious recipes, and began to dabble with cheese making. This "dabbling" became the world-renowned cheese maker Cypress Grove Chevre. Her most famous and award-winning cheese, Humboldt Fog, is a creamy yet crumbly cake of sweet goat's milk with a layer of vegetable ash through the center.

The Wild Honey–Syrah Syrup should be used sparingly, a drizzle of molten sweetness to contrast the tang of warm goat cheese.

cont'd

PUFF PASTRY PILLOWS WITH HUMBOLDT FOG, RED ONION, AND WILD HONEY—SYRAH SYRUP

SERVES 8

FOR THE WILD HONEY–SYRAH SYRUP

1½ cups/360 ml Syrah or other full-bodied red wine

½ cup/120 ml wildflower honey

FOR THE PASTRY

1 sheet puff pastry

½ red onion

8 oz/225 g Humboldt Fog or other soft, mild goat cheese

¼ cup/15 g chopped fresh flat-leaf parsley

TO PREPARE THE SYRUP: Combine the ingredients in a medium saucepan and gently bring to a simmer over low heat, whisking from time to time. Reduce by half, 25 to 30 minutes, or until the syrup coats the back of a spoon. Remove from the heat and let cool. The syrup can be stored in a tightly sealed container for up to 1 month in the refrigerator. Bring to room temperature or heat gently before serving.

TO PREPARE THE PASTRY: Preheat the oven to 400°F/ 200°C/gas 6.

Line a baking sheet/tray with parchment/baking paper.

Cut the sheet of pastry into eight rectangles using a fluted pasta cutter or sharp knife. Slice the onion into paper-thin rings, using a mandoline, or very sharp knife. Place the rings in a bowl of cold water until ready to use.

Crumble the goat cheese over the pastry tiles, leaving about a ¼-in/6-mm border. Drain the onion slices, pat dry with paper towels, and scatter over the tarts, followed by the chopped parsley.

Bake for 15 to 20 minutes, or until the pastry puffs nicely and the goat cheese is golden. A few burned spots here and there are preferable. Remove from the heat and serve hot, drizzled with the syrup.

WHITE WINE: Riesling
RED WINE: Chinon

GOUGÈRES

MAKES ABOUT 15 GOUGÈRES

6 tbsp/85 g unsalted butter

⅞ cup/210 ml water

⅔ cup/80 g all-purpose/plain flour

3 eggs

4 oz/115 g best-quality Gruyère or Comté cheese

A pinch of salt

Traditionally from Burgundy, gougères are actually made with the great Gruyère de Comté from the Jura Mountains. How the Alpine cheese found its way into a classic Burgundian recipe seems less important here than how delicious these savory little puffs are.

Look for the very best Gruyère you can get your hands on for this recipe; my favorite is the twenty-month-old Gruyère de Comté from Chantal Plasse. Deep caramel flavors and wonderful crystallized lactose sugars will have you snacking on as much cheese as you'll use in this recipe.

Preheat the oven to 400°F/200°C/gas 6.

In a small saucepan over medium heat, heat the butter and water together until the butter is melted. Bring to a boil, whisking to combine. Continue whisking as you add the flour all at once, stirring constantly until a shiny dough forms. Continue cooking over medium heat for 2 to 3 minutes, stirring constantly to evaporate excess moisture.

Remove from the heat and transfer the dough mixture to the bowl of an electric mixer fitted with the whisk attachment. Turn on the machine to medium speed and add the eggs. Continue to mix until the dough is smooth and the eggs are incorporated. Turn the machine off and add half of the cheese. Turn the mixer back on and continue mixing, until the cheese is blended, and then add the remaining cheese and the salt.

Line a baking sheet/tray with parchment/baking paper. Using a pastry/piping bag with a plain tip, pipe the dough into small mounds about the size of a golf ball, about 2 in/ 5 cm apart.

Bake for 25 to 30 minutes, or until puffed and golden. Serve hot, or let cool completely before refrigerating or freezing, after which the gougères can be reheated in a 350°F/180°C/gas 4 oven until piping hot.

WINE: Burgundy, white or red

This is a savory version of the ricotta fritters with chocolate that I had in Rome many years ago. They are lighter than a rice-based fritter, like *suppli*, and are fantastic with a glass of Prosecco or other sparking wine before dinner.

Heat the oil to 360°F/180°C in a deep fryer or heavy saucepan. In a medium bowl, mix together the ricotta, eggs, pecorino, flour, lemon zest, and parsley. Stir in a pinch of salt and a few grindings of pepper.

Make balls of the ricotta mixture about the size of golf balls. Dredge the ricotta balls in the extra flour and fry until golden brown, about 2 minutes.

Drain on paper towels or paper bags and serve immediately.

. . . .

WHITE WINE: Kerner, Chenin Blanc, Savennières

SAVORY LEMON, RICOTTA, AND PECORINO FRITTERS

MAKES 10 TO 12 FRITTERS

2 cups/480 ml pure olive oil for frying

1 lb/455 g fresh ricotta cheese

4 eggs, beaten

¼ cup/25 g grated Pecorino Romano cheese

¾ cup/90 g all-purpose/plain flour, plus extra for dredging

Zest of 1 lemon

1 tbsp fresh flat-leaf parsley, chopped fine

Salt and freshly cracked black pepper

I found one of my favorite books almost twenty years ago at the tiny Italian language bookshop, Cavalli, tucked behind a bus stop in San Francisco's iconic North Beach neighborhood. I used to peruse the shelves of Italian books and magazines there, well before I learned to speak the language, and there I discovered the treasure chest of recipes in *Le Ricette Regionali Italiane* by Anna Gosetti della Salda. A massive tome of the most authentic dishes I have ever found, including a fantastic recipe for frog risotto!

The following recipe is one found in that book, made easier these days by the availability of great Italian cheeses. The original calls for Robioletta, though, in this case, I love the use of a sheep's and cow's milks cheese from Italy's Langhe countryside, Robiola due latte.

Combine the basil, celery leaves, parsley, and garlic in a large mortar. Add a pinch of salt and a crack of pepper and grind to a rough paste.

Squeeze the lemon juice into the paste and add the olive oil. Mix well and then taste. If the lemon is too pronounced, add a bit more oil. There should be a nice balance of fruity flavor, herbal aroma, and lemony tang.

Add the entire piece of Robiola, rind and all, and work into a smooth and creamy paste with the pestle. Season well with salt, pepper, and more oil or lemon juice as desired.

Serve Robiola Verde as you would a good guacamole, with pieces of focaccia in place of chips.

WHITE WINE: Gavi di Gavi
RED WINE: gentle Nebbiolo (not Barolo), Dolcetto

ROBIOLA VERDE

SERVES 4 TO 6

10 fresh basil leaves

5 fresh celery leaves

½ cup/30 g fresh flat-leaf parsley

2 garlic cloves, peeled

Salt and freshly cracked black pepper

1 tbsp freshly squeezed lemon juice, plus more if needed

2 tbsp extra-virgin olive oil, plus more if needed

One 8 oz/225 g square Robiola due latte cheese

Focaccia or other flatbread, for serving

TWICE-BAKED TRUFFLE TREMOR SOUFFLÉ

SERVES 2

4 tbsp butter

1 cup/240 ml whole milk

¼ cup/30 g all-purpose/plain flour

1 bay leaf

Salt and white pepper

2 eggs separated; yolks well beaten, plus 1 egg white

2 oz/55 g Truffle Tremor goat cheese, rind removed and crumbled

⅜ cup/90 ml heavy/double cream

2 tbsp grated Parmigiano-Reggiano cheese

Here is an increasingly popular way to have your soufflé and eat it, too. The convenience of double baking has made the serving of a soufflé at dinner parties much less intimidating. Truffle Tremor is an inspired goat's milk cheese, once again from revolutionary cheese master Mary Keehn at Cypress Grove Chevre in Northern California. In this case, fresh Humboldt County goat's milk is laced with black summer truffles, whose perfume explodes when heated.

Preheat the oven to 325°F/165°C/gas 3.

Grease two ramekins or individual soufflé dishes with 1 tbsp of the butter.

In a medium saucepan, gently bring the milk to a simmer over low heat, and then turn off the heat.

Melt the remaining butter in a large saucepan. Add the flour, whisking constantly, and continue to cook over medium heat for about 3 minutes. Remove from the heat and add the milk, a little at first, whisking constantly. Add the bay leaf and then season with salt and pepper. Reduce the heat to a simmer and cook for 10 to 12 minutes. Remove from the heat and let cool to room temperature.

When the sauce is completely cooled, whisk in the egg yolks. Scatter the goat cheese over the surface of the sauce and then fold in.

In a clean, dry bowl, whisk the egg whites with a pinch of salt until stiff. Fold one-third of the beaten egg whites into the sauce to loosen it slightly and then quickly fold in the remaining whites.

Fill the prepared ramekins almost to the brim, place in a baking pan, and fill the pan with enough boiling water to come about two-thirds of the way up the sides of the ramekins. Carefully place the pan on the middle rack of the oven and bake for about 15 minutes, or until the soufflés have risen and are firm to the touch.

Remove from the oven and let sit in the water bath for 10 to 15 minutes. (The soufflés can be made to this point up to a day in advance; remove the ramekins from the water bath, cover with plastic wrap/cling film, and refrigerate.)

When ready to serve, preheat the oven to 475°F/240°C/gas 9.

Gently transfer the soufflés to individual ovenproof plates by turning them upside down directly onto the plates. Lift off the ramekins. Pour 3 tbsp cream over and around each soufflé and sprinkle with 1 tbsp Parmigiano cheese. Bake for 6 to 7 minutes, or until deep golden brown and piping hot. Serve immediately.

WHITE WINE: Chenin Blanc
RED WINE: Barolo, Pinot Noir, Chinon

CREAM OF CELERY ROOT SOUP WITH BLU DI BUFALA AND PEARS / 69

CHILLED CUCUMBER SOUP WITH SHEEP'S MILK FROMAGE BLANC / 71

ROASTED GARLIC AND CAULIFLOWER SOUP WITH AGED CHEDDAR / 72

FARRO AND WHITE BEAN SOUP WITH REGGIANO RINDS / 73

ASPARAGUS SOUP WITH GOAT CHEESE CROSTINI
AND FRIED SHALLOTS / 75

ROMAN EGG-DROP SOUP / 76

MONASTIC FISH AND
TOMATO SOUP WITH PARMIGIANO-REGGIANO / 79

SOUPS

Recipes for soups can seem antithetical to the great soups of many cultures, which often defy the very concept of a set list of specific ingredients. I think of the ancient medieval kitchens of Europe, in which massive "eternal" cauldrons were kept going around the clock. If one wanted to cook a piece of meat, you simply popped it in the pot with all of the other things and fished it out when it was done, leaving the broth that much the better.

From minestrone to chicken soup, foraging through the refrigerator and pantry for things to add to a soup is half the fun of making it. "Oh, an onion!" or "Look! A bag of dried cannellini beans!" or "Are those the drippings from last night's roasted chicken I wisely saved?"

Still, there are some elegant preparations and simple, satisfying soups that are nice to be able to re-create, and in the case of making soups with cheese, I'd like to point you in the general direction of some of the great possibilities. Just remember: especially with soups, use what is in season and be true to your own desires over being true to any recipe.

WINE NOTE

If a soup is served while the white wine is still pouring (and rarely does one buy wine for the soup course), then a medium-body white with a balance of earth and fruit is a great template in general. Some basic guidelines for specific soup types and their wine complements are:

- For tomato soups, serve crisp white wines from Sauvignon Blanc to Provençal Rosé.

- For asparagus soups, serve less fruit-driven wines such as Grüner Veltliner and whites from the Alto Adige.

- For bean and pasta soups, serve rich wines with balance, including Bergerac Sec, Cahors, and Cannonau.

This is a wonderful soup for later in the year, when the hearty texture of celery root and potatoes matches the autumn mood, perhaps garnished with pieces of wheat bread cut into leaf shapes and toasted with a touch of butter! It is a fairly rich soup, but the pears give a nice balance to the elegant combination of flavors.

Blu di Bufala is a rare find of water buffalo's milk blue cheese from Lombardy, but Roquefort or Stilton can easily be substituted.

Heat the olive oil in a large pot over low heat. Add the onion and garlic and sweat without coloring, about 10 minutes. Add the celery root, potatoes, stock, and bay leaf. Season with salt and pepper. Bring to a rapid boil and then reduce the heat to low; simmer, covered, for about 1 hour, or until the celery root is very tender and cooked through.

Let cool completely and remove the bay leaf. Add the pears, cheese, and cream, stirring well to combine.

In a food processor fitted with the blade attachment, puree the soup in batches until smooth. Strain through a mesh sieve into a clean pot. Gently reheat the soup and serve hot.

CREAM OF CELERY ROOT SOUP WITH BLU DI BUFALA AND PEARS

SERVES 6

2 tbsp extra-virgin olive oil

1 medium yellow onion, chopped

2 garlic cloves, peeled

4 lb/1.8 kg celery root, peeled and cut into thin slices

8 oz/225 g russet potatoes, peeled and diced

4 cups/960 ml best-quality chicken or vegetable stock

1 bay leaf

Salt and white pepper

3 very ripe Anjou or Bartlett/Williams' pears, peeled, cored, and chopped

6 oz/170 g Blu di Bufala, Roquefort, or Stilton cheese

1½ cups/360 ml heavy/double cream

Think green gazpacho on a hot summer day. I love the sweet creamy flavors of Spanish sheep's milk fromage blanc, which I also devour on toast with homemade marmalade. This recipe also works nicely with cow's milk fromage blanc or even crème fraîche.

A tin of smoked paprika from Spain is indispensable in the pantry, and the smoky kick it lends to this soup is vital.

In a food processor fitted with the blade attachment, pulse the cucumbers, onion, and mint to a smooth puree. Add the fromage blanc and season with salt and pepper. Pulse a few more times to combine. Transfer to a container, cover, and chill for at least 30 minutes before serving.

Divide the soup among chilled soup bowls or cups and sprinkle the tops with a pinch of smoked paprika. Garnish with fresh mint and serve cold.

CHILLED CUCUMBER SOUP WITH SHEEP'S MILK FROMAGE BLANC

SERVES 4

2 lb/910 g cucumbers, peeled and seeded

½ small red onion, chopped

½ cup/30 g fresh mint leaves, plus extra for garnish

8 oz/225 g sheep's milk fromage blanc

Salt and freshly cracked black pepper

Smoked paprika for sprinkling

ROASTED GARLIC AND CAULIFLOWER SOUP WITH AGED CHEDDAR

SERVES 4

FOR THE ROASTED GARLIC CHICKEN BROTH

6 whole garlic heads, unpeeled

1 tbsp extra-virgin olive oil

1¼ cups/280 ml chicken stock

FOR THE SOUP

2 tbsp unsalted butter

1 medium yellow onion, chopped

1 head cauliflower, broken into florets

¼ cup/30 g all-purpose/plain flour

2½ cups/600 ml whole milk

1½ cups/225 g grated aged cow's milk Cheddar cheese

Salt and freshly cracked black pepper

This soup was born of a desire to not waste the rich flavors of roasted garlic from making the Goat Cheese and Roasted Garlic Beehive (page 29). The roasted garlic skins are simmered in chicken stock to carry their perfume over into this decadent soup. If you happen to have made the Beehive, simply use the skins left over from six of the garlic bulbs. Otherwise, follow the directions below.

TO PREPARE THE BROTH: Preheat the oven to 400°F/200°C/gas 6.

Spread the garlic on a baking sheet/tray and toss with the olive oil. Bake on the oven's middle rack for 35 to 40 minutes, or until deep golden brown with burn spots here and there. Being careful not to burn your fingers, give the garlic heads a pinch. They should be very soft. Let the garlic cool to room temperature and then cut the heads in half horizontally with a serrated bread knife.

Squeeze the roasted garlic pulp into a bowl. Mix the garlic pulp with a whisk until smooth.

Put the roasted garlic peels and pulp in a medium pot along with the stock. Bring to a boil and then reduce the heat and simmer for 20 minutes. Strain the stock and discard the garlic peels. Proceed with making the soup.

TO PREPARE THE SOUP: Melt the butter in large saucepan over medium heat. Add the onion and sauté for about 10 minutes, or until tender. Add the cauliflower and roasted garlic–infused chicken broth. Bring to a boil and then reduce the heat and simmer, covered, for 12 to 15 minutes, or until the cauliflower is tender.

In a separate pan, combine the flour and milk, whisking constantly until smooth. Add to the soup and cook over medium heat, stirring constantly for 5 to 7 minutes, or until the soup begins to bubble and thicken. Remove from the heat.

Add the cheese all at once and stir until melted and smooth. Season with salt and pepper and serve.

In soups, the addition of rinds left over from grating Parmigiano-Reggiano goes beyond the obvious tendency of Italian home cooks to leave nothing to waste. There is a richness imparted to long-simmering soups as the rind slowly breaks down. The use of cheese rinds in slow cooking also results in the need for less salt to be added. Save rinds wrapped in foil and then in an airtight plastic bag in the cheese drawer of your refrigerator. They can also be used in ragù and meat stews.

One might assume that what is left of the rind after cooking should be left out of the serving bowl. But I actually love the rustic look and that unmistakable real Parmigiano-Reggiano stamp, so I will break the rind into as many pieces as there are guests to ensure everyone receives a piece!

Drain and rinse the cannellini and farro beans.

Heat the olive oil in a large pot over low heat. Add the pancetta and cook for 10 to 15 minutes, until it just begins to crisp. Remove the pancetta from the pan and set aside, leaving the fat in the pan. Add the onion, carrots, and celery. Turn up the heat to medium-high and cook for 5 minutes or so, until the vegetables begin to get a little color. Add the garlic and cook for 5 minutes more. Season with salt and pepper. Add the rosemary, tomatoes, and cannellini beans. Add just enough cold water to cover the ingredients, along with the Parmigiano rinds. Bring to a boil and then reduce the heat to a steady simmer. Cook for about an hour, skimming off any scum from the surface. Continue to add water to the soup as it cooks and the beans swell.

Add the farro and continue cooking until the beans are completely soft—about another hour. Season with plenty of salt and pepper.

Serve drizzled with plenty of extra-virgin olive oil.

FARRO AND WHITE BEAN SOUP WITH REGGIANO RINDS

SERVES 6

2 cups/450 g dried cannellini beans, soaked overnight

2 cups/400 g farro, soaked for 2 hours

3 tbsp extra-virgin olive oil, plus more for drizzling

4 oz/115 g pancetta

1 large onion, finely chopped

2 carrots, peeled and chopped

2 stalks celery, chopped

2 garlic cloves, peeled

Salt and freshly cracked black pepper

1 sprig rosemary

14 oz/400 g fresh or best-quality canned tomatoes, peeled and chopped

1 lb/455 g Parmigiano-Reggiano cheese rinds

This soup has a silky texture that contrasts nicely with the crunchy crostini and caramelized shallots that float atop it. The tang of goat cheese—whether a fresh Robiola or a simple farm chèvre—is a nice way to cut some of the richness of the creamy soup.

TO PREPARE THE SOUP: In a 4-quart/3.8-L pot over medium-low heat, melt the butter. Add the onion and cook for about 10 minutes, or until softened and just starting to gild.

Trim the asparagus of any overly woody ends. Add to the onion and season well with salt and pepper. Cook for 5 to 10 minutes, or until the asparagus turns a brilliant green. Add the stock, bring to a simmer, and cook, covered, for 30 minutes.

Let the soup cool a bit before pureeing, either with a wand blender or in batches using a food processor fitted with the blade attachment. Be careful pureeing if the soup is very hot.

Return the soup to a clean pan and stir in the cream. Bring to a boil and cook for 5 minutes more. Add the lemon juice and season with more salt and pepper.

TO PREPARE THE CROSTINI AND SHALLOTS: Preheat the oven to 400°F/200°C/gas 6. Cut the baguette into ⅛-in/3-mm slices. Lay the slices out on a baking sheet/tray and drizzle with 2 tbsp of the olive oil. Bake for 10 to 12 minutes, or until golden and crispy. Remove and let cool.

Heat the remaining oil in a sauté pan over medium-high heat. Add the shallots and fry, until deep golden brown and crunchy, about 2 minutes. Spread the goat cheese on the crostini.

Pour the hot soup into warm soup bowls and lay the crostini to float in the center of the soup. Place the caramelized shallots in the center of the goat cheese crostini and serve immediately.

ASPARAGUS SOUP WITH GOAT CHEESE CROSTINI AND FRIED SHALLOTS

SERVES 6

FOR THE SOUP
3 tbsp unsalted butter

1 large onion, chopped

2 lb/910 g medium asparagus spears

Salt and white pepper

5 cups/1.2 L best-quality chicken stock, vegetable stock, or water

½ cup/120 ml heavy/double cream

1 tsp freshly squeezed lemon juice

FOR THE CROSTINI AND SHALLOTS
½ French baguette

6 tbsp/90 ml extra-virgin olive oil

4 large shallots

6 oz/170 g fresh goat cheese

ROMAN EGG-DROP SOUP

SERVES 4

4½ cups/1 L best-quality chicken stock

3 eggs

3½ oz/100 g Parmigiano-Reggiano, grated

½ cup/30 g finely chopped fresh flat-leaf parsley

Salt and freshly cracked black pepper

Fresh nutmeg

This classic Roman soup known as *stracciatella* (meaning, literally, "little rags") is a perfect example of taking very good ingredients and doing very little to them. Whether homemade or store bought, the highest-quality chicken stock is vital, as is sourcing very good eggs. The technique is fairly simple, but it is important not to break up the eggs too early, which will result in a messy scrambled egg soup with cheese and parsley.

In a large pot, bring the stock to a rapid boil.

Meanwhile, whisk together the eggs, cheese, and parsley in a medium bowl. Season with salt, pepper, and a grating or two of nutmeg. When the stock is boiling, pour the egg and cheese mixture into the pot all at once and do not touch for the first minute or so. Then lightly stir the cooked egg with a fork so that it separates into large, uneven "rags." Serve immediately.

Here is another Italian version of the egg-drop soup (see page 76). This one comes to us from the great Pellegrino Artusi in his highly influential book *Science in the Kitchen and the Art of Eating Well*, first published in 1891.

He tells of a Tuscan duke who sent his cooks to the Arthurian monastery where this soup was created to learn the recipe. Although the cooks returned able to produce a delicious version, the good monks hadn't shared the real secret to the deep flavors of such a simple soup: the use of capon broth instead of water. If you are savvy enough to make a proper capon broth, then all the better, but it is a delicious soup with a good-quality chicken broth, too.

In a deep sauté pan large enough to hold all of the ingredients, heat ¼ cup/60 ml of the olive oil over medium heat and sauté the onion and celery for 10 to 12 minutes, or until golden. Add the fish and parsley. Season well with salt and pepper. Add the tomatoes to cover the fish and simmer for 7 to 10 minutes, or until the fish is tender and cooked through. Add the broth and bring to a simmer. Adjust the seasoning and then strain the soup through a mesh sieve over another pot or large bowl, pressing the fish and vegetables through the sieve with the back of a spoon or rubber spatula. Discard the solids.

Return the strained soup to the pan, bring to a boil, and then turn off the heat.

Meanwhile, in a large soup tureen or serving bowl, break the eggs and beat well with a fork. Add the Parmigiano and stir to combine.

Pour the very hot soup over the egg and cheese mixture and stir well.

Fry the bread in the remaining ½ cup/120 ml olive oil over medium-high heat for 3 to 4 minutes, or until golden, and then distribute equally among the serving bowls. Ladle the hot soup over the fried bread cubes and serve immediately.

MONASTIC FISH AND TOMATO SOUP WITH PARMIGIANO-REGGIANO

SERVES 4 TO 6

¾ cup/180 ml extra-virgin olive oil

1 small yellow onion, chopped fine

2 stalks celery or fennel bulb, chopped fine

1 lb/455 g fresh fish fillet such as sole, trout, or any other mild whitefish, bones intact if available

2 tbsp roughly chopped fresh flat-leaf parsley

Salt and white pepper

12¼ oz/350 g fresh ripe tomatoes (or best-quality canned tomatoes), peeled and chopped

4 cups/960 ml good-quality capon broth, chicken broth, or water

3 eggs

6 tbsp/40 g finely grated Parmigiano-Reggiano cheese

2 cups/170 g small cubes crusty Italian style bread

APPLE AND CELERY SALAD WITH CHÈVRE NOIR AND HAZELNUTS / 83

BABY LETTUCES WITH STRAWBERRIES,
ROCAMADOUR, AND WALNUT OIL / 85

LEONORA GOAT CHEESE WITH
BABY ARUGULA AND PINK GRAPEFRUIT / 86

FRISÉE WITH CHÈVRE CHAUD / 87

CABBAGE SLAW WITH SMOKEY BLUE / 89

FRESH PEACHES WITH HEIRLOOM TOMATOES AND BURRATA / 91

SALADS

The Romans are famous for maintaining that it takes four
people to make a salad properly: a wise man to add the salt,
a miser to add the vinegar, a tightwad to add the oil, and a
madman to toss it all together.

The right balance of dressing to greens is an extremely personal matter. There is no correct amount for everyone, and,
when it comes to salads, I often place extra-virgin olive oil,
vinegar or citrus fruits, and cracked pepper on the table,
encouraging my guests to accommodate themselves. The
world probably could do without another recipe for Caesar
salad or insalata caprese, as those classics are set in a kind
of culinary stone that needs little chiseling. Still, there is
always room to play, and if one is guided by the seasons and
finds what is at its best from the local cheese counter, some
surprisingly new doors may open.

I must admit that my favorite salads are simple. Often they
are little more than a handful of wild arugula/rocket with a
drizzle of fruity extra-virgin olive oil and a squeeze of Meyer
lemon from our prolific backyard tree. But cheeses of all
kinds are a great way to play with contrasts of textures and
flavors. While rarely the main ingredient in salads, the right
cheese can unite the various components and often will
become that precious jewel we find ourselves secretly search-
ing for in the treasure chest in hopes of finding more.

WINE NOTE

If the salad precedes the main course, as is often the case, the vinegar or citrus juices in the dressing will look for higher-tone white wines like Sauvignon Blanc and Trebbiano to echo their brightness. Additionally, bitter greens such as arugula/rocket, radicchio, and endive, as well as many leafy vegetables, contain flavors that seek balance; wines like Soave, Gavi di Gavi, Verdicchio, and Kerner that tend to be crisp in nature easily accomplish this. Richer, softer, fruity wines will lose these very dimensions when paired with bitter greens. When tomatoes are the feature of the salad, look for brighter, more mineral-driven whites such as Grüner Veltliner, Sancerre, white Bordeaux, and wonderful Txakoli from the Basque Country. Certain earthy red wines like Sangiovese and Rioja can pair nicely with tomatoes as well.

In the European context, salad is served after the main course, while the fats from the main dish are still on the palette. In this case, an open bottle of red wine is probably already on the table. Fortunately, main-course red wines often have structural characteristics that balance the acids in citrus fruits and lend themselves well to salads and their dressings.

Chèvre noir is a delicious, two-year-aged goat's milk "cheddar" from Chesterville, Canada (no relation!). It is at first Cheddar-like, and then it tastes "goaty," which is why I suppose, like goat's milk Gouda, it is such a popular cheese for so many different people. When I'm on the go, I find a chunk of chèvre noir and a crisp, sweet, in-season apple to be the perfect snack . . . well, I suppose perfect would involve a bit of salami, too!

This is a light and crunchy salad that champions the credo "take very good ingredients and do very little to them."

Wash the celery well. Pull away the outer stalks to get to the pale green interior stalks. (Save the outer stalks for soups or stocks.) Separate the interior stalks, leaves intact, and slice on an angle, ⅛ in/3 mm thick.

Fill a medium mixing bowl with cold water. Squeeze the half lemon into the water to acidulate it. This will prevent the apples from oxidizing.

Peel, quarter, and core the apples. Cut each quarter into ¼-in-/6-mm-thick slices. Place the apple slices directly into the lemon water as you cut them.

In a small bowl, whisk together the honey, olive oil, ¼ cup/60 ml lemon juice, and shallot. Dry the apple slices on a clean kitchen towel.

Place the celery, apple slices, and cheese in a large mixing bowl. Add the hazelnuts and then the honey–olive oil dressing. Season with plenty of pepper and serve.

APPLE AND CELERY SALAD WITH CHÈVRE NOIR AND HAZELNUTS

SERVES 4

1 medium bunch celery

½ lemon, plus ¼ cup/60 ml freshly squeezed lemon juice

2 large, crisp Pink Lady, Honey Crisp, or Gala apples

4 tsp wildflower honey

⅔ cup/165 ml extra-virgin olive oil

1 large shallot, minced

¼ lb/115 g chèvre noir or other goat's milk Cheddar, shaved into thin slices

¾ cup/130 g roughly chopped hazelnuts, toasted

Freshly cracked black pepper

I had this fabulous and refreshing salad in the postcard-perfect village of Domme in the Périgord of southwestern France. The view of the Dordogne River from this bastide hamlet stretches as far as the eye can see and is truly something out of a fairy tale. This is also foie gras country, and the beloved delicacy is to be had in an overabundance at times. One café actually placed individual toasters at every table, so that guests could toast their own slices of pain-de-mie for the thick slabs of foie gras sprinkled with coarse salt served for lunch.

This salad came as a welcome relief from the daily intake of confit and foie gras. It is a delightful summer lunch in and of itself. If Rocamadour is unavailable, Bocconcini di Pura Capra or another young goat cheese will do nicely.

In a small bowl, whisk together the shallot, verjuice, and walnut oil. Season with salt and pepper.

Dress the greens in a large bowl. Arrange on four individual salad plates. Divide the strawberries and radishes among the salads. Top each salad with a whole disc of Rocamadour and serve with plenty of fresh baguette.

BABY LETTUCES WITH STRAWBERRIES, ROCAMADOUR, AND WALNUT OIL

SERVES 4

1 shallot, minced

2 tsp verjuice

2 tsp walnut oil

Salt and freshly cracked black pepper

4 cups/170 g loosely packed fresh baby lettuces, washed and dried

12 fresh and very ripe strawberries, stemmed and sliced

2 radishes, cut into paper-thin slices

4 discs ripe Rocamadour cheese

1 baguette

LEONORA GOAT CHEESE WITH BABY ARUGULA AND PINK GRAPEFRUIT

SERVES 4 TO 6

3¾ cups/115 g baby arugula/rocket

2 large ruby red grapefruits at the peak of season, sectioned and kept in their own juice

½ cup/120 ml best-quality extra-virgin olive oil (I love the fine oils from Italy's Puglia region for salads like this.)

6 oz/170 g Leonora or other crumbly goat cheese

Nasturtiums or edible pansies (optional)

This deconstructed salad is a classic example of necessity as the mother of invention. My wife and I were serving a brunch buffet celebrating our son's third birthday (sugary scones and honey-soaked muffins really get a toddler party started). I had the nagging suspicion that something light and seemingly healthful should be prepared for the adults. Dressing a salad for a large group, especially for buffet service, is always tricky. For this occasion, a platter of baby arugula/rocket was topped with nasturtiums from the garden and crumbled Leonora cheese.

With a cake-like texture, Leonora is made from the milk of the cheese maker's own goat herd on a farmstead in the mountains above Leon. Only recently available in the United States, the cheese is quickly becoming one of my top picks. Leonora is a delightful fresh goat cheese and is equally at home on a cheese board, especially if a little cherry tomato jam (see page 37) happens to be around!

Tart grapefruit juice is the perfect acid to the rich olive oil and goat cheese, and allowing guests to dress the salad as they go keeps things bright and avoids the dilemma of a wilted salad.

Arrange the arugula/rocket on a large, flat platter. Place the grapefruit segments in a small bowl in the center of the arugula/rocket. Include the extra-virgin olive oil in a cruet for self-serving. Crumble the goat cheese over the arugula/rocket and scatter the flowers over the salad to serve.

Warm goat cheese is one of my favorite little luxuries in life, whether spread on a slice of baguette and heated under the broiler/grill for a moment or rolled in bread crumbs and quickly fried, as in this simple and classic preparation.

Any greens may be used, depending on the season, but the sweet crunch of frisée, not to mention the beautiful colors, is a classic fit for these little buttons of crispy, creamy goat cheese.

Cut or form the goat cheese into eight rounds. Place the bread crumbs in a dish and add a pinch of salt and a little pepper. Beat the egg in another dish.

Heat the olive oil in a nonstick frying pan over medium-high heat. Dip each cheese round into the egg and then into the bread crumbs, and then add it to the hot oil. Fry for about 3 minutes, or until golden brown on one side; flip and fry until golden brown on the other side, 2 to 3 minutes more.

Meanwhile, place the vinegar, mustard, and shallot in a salad bowl and whisk until combined. Add the walnut oil, little by little, until emulsified. Season the vinaigrette with salt and pepper.

Put the frisée in a bowl and toss to coat with the vinaigrette. Divide the frisée among eight salad plates and place one goat cheese round on each plate to serve.

FRISÉE WITH CHÈVRE CHAUD

SERVES 8

8 oz/225 g fresh goat cheese

½ cup/40 g panko bread crumbs

Salt and freshly cracked black pepper

1 egg

2 tbsp extra-virgin olive oil

2 tbsp red wine vinegar

1 tbsp Dijon mustard

1 shallot, minced

6 tbsp/90 ml walnut oil

1 head frisée lettuce, cleaned and separated

Cary Bryant and David Gremmels at Rogue Creamery in Central Point, Oregon, were the first artisan cheese makers to smoke blue cheese—something that someone should have done a long time ago. Raw–cow's milk blue is smoked over hazelnut shells for 16 hours, and the results are transcendent. I love it on a cheeseburger as much as I do in this bright and tasty take on coleslaw.

In a food processor fitted with the blade attachment, combine the buttermilk, honey, blue cheese, and vinegar. Blend until smooth. Taste for tangy to sweet ratio and adjust with the vinegar and honey accordingly. Place the cabbage and onion in a large bowl. Season with plenty of pepper. Add the dressing and mix until the cabbage is well dressed. The slaw is best if it is allowed to chill and mingle. It can be made the night before serving.

CABBAGE SLAW WITH SMOKEY BLUE

SERVES 6 TO 8

½ cup/120 ml buttermilk

3 tbsp wildflower honey, plus more if needed

½ lb/225 g Smokey Blue cheese

¼ cup/60 ml sherry vinegar, plus more if needed

12 cups/3 kg finely shredded red and green cabbage

1 small red onion, cut into paper-thin slices

Freshly cracked black pepper

First invented in 1920 on the Bianchini farm in Puglia, Burrata has experienced a renaissance of massive proportions in the last few years. Basically, it is a pouch of fresh mozzarella filled with "rags" of left-over mozzarella and cream. It is traditionally wrapped in the leaves of asphodel (a plant that, according to Greek mythology, is the favorite food of the dead, while Burrata could arguably be a favorite of most of us living!).

Today the cheese is available not only in Italy, but many mozzarella makers abroad have succeeded in making some very worthy versions. Generally served as is with perhaps a splash of extra-virgin olive oil and a few raw arugula/rocket leaves, it is a highly versatile cheese in the kitchen. In this case, vine-ripened tomatoes and sugar-sweet peaches are married with the fresh Burrata for a bright summer salad in which both fruits enjoy the limelight.

Arrange the tomatoes and peaches in an alternating pattern on a large serving platter.

With your fingers, tear the Burrata into large golf ball–size pieces and scatter them over the tomatoes and peaches. Scatter the onion slices over the salad, followed by the basil. Season with plenty of pepper, drizzle the entire dish with the olive oil, and serve.

ALTERNATE VERSION
Replace the heirloom tomato with 4 cups/680 g cherry tomatoes and replace the peaches with 1 lb/455 g pitted and halved black cherries. Mix the tomatoes and black cherries in a bowl along with the onion, basil, and pepper. Cut the Burrata in half and arrange on a platter with the tomato-cherry salad atop and around the Burrata halves.

FRESH PEACHES WITH HEIRLOOM TOMATOES AND BURRATA

SERVES 4 TO 6

2 large, ripe heirloom tomatoes, cored and cut into ¼-in-/6-mm-thick slices

4 large, ripe but firm peaches, pitted and cut into ¼-in-/6-mm-thick wedges

1 lb/455 g fresh Burrata cheese

½ red onion, cut into paper-thin slices

¼ cup/15 g torn fresh basil

Freshly cracked black pepper

¼ cup/60 ml extra-virgin olive oil

TARTIFLETTE / 95

POTATO GRATIN WITH BLACK TRUFFLE CHEESE AND FRESH THYME / 96

TWICE-BAKED POTATOES WITH MIDNIGHT MOON GOAT CHEESE / 97

ASPARAGUS AND POTATO FRITTERS WITH
MANOURI CHEESE, CHILIES, AND MINT / 98

ZUCCHINI AND GOAT GOUDA FRITTERS / 99

FRIED ZUCCHINI BLOSSOMS WITH TOMME
DE MA GRANDE-MÈRE AND CITRUS HONEY / 100

ROASTED BUTTERNUT SQUASH WITH
FRESH TUSCAN PECORINO AND DEVIL'S HONEY / 102

BROCCOLINI WITH CARAMELIZED SHALLOTS AND
SICILIAN PECORINO WITH SAFFRON / 105

GOLDEN EGGPLANT WITH
CREAMY FRENCH FETA AND CROUTONS / 107

GRILLED RADICCHIO WITH SMOKED PROVOLONE AND PANCETTA / 109

VEGETABLES

I found this chapter the most difficult to whittle down. Although I, myself, could never give up eating certain cured pork products and various other gifts from the animal kingdom, I find the plethora of ways in which to unite vegetables and cheese overwhelming. The explosion of farmers' markets and high-quality produce available at the local grocery store is awe inspiring, giving us all a chance to return to eating food in season and at the peak of flavor.

And then there is the home garden. I used to insist that I had a "black thumb;" anything I tried to grow would inevitably die from obsessive over-watering or total neglect as the days got busy. But I recently decided to give it another go. Spurred on by the enthusiasm of my three-year-old son, I began reviving my hard-to-kill rosemary and other herbs with great success. After that, I graduated to raised garden beds filled with blackberries, Yukon gold potatoes, rainbow radishes, tomatoes, artichokes, strawberries, and even pepperoncini to dry for use on pastas. The joy of watching my son race into the kitchen with plump blackberries glistening with juices so that we can make "jelly" by simply smashing it with a fork and spreading on a biscuit is a reward I never imagined.

Even if it is merely a pot of fresh basil growing in an old coffee can on the windowsill, fresh mozzarella cut into thick slices has no greater friend than those perfumed leaves roughly torn and scattered on top, united with an anointing of extra-virgin olive oil. It is a kind of holy trinity that can be experienced incarnate everyday.

WINE NOTE

In a family-style setting, I look to the entrées that vegetable dishes accompany to better inform the wine selection. But consider, as always, something of medium weight—neither too light nor too heavy—in whites or reds.

Certain types of vegetables contain enzymes that can kill the fruit in wine, narrowing the variety of wines that go with things like asparagus and artichokes. Combining cheese with these wine-unfriendly foods bridges that gap, as the richness in the cheese opens up a multitude of possibilities for wine pairings.

In general, for uncooked vegetables, I find that lean, crisp white wines match more closely. But when vegetables are cooked, enzymes and acids are neutralized, so the vegetables lend themselves to richer whites and heavier reds. Take a bite of raw asparagus; you can't put a single red wine with it. Put that asparagus on a hot grill for a few minutes, though—the natural sugars caramelize and, suddenly, most red wines become good pairings.

Tartiflette is said to be a fairly recent invention by a few marketing geniuses to help sales of Reblochon cheese in France. Provenance aside, the classic combination of potatoes, bacon, wine, and melted cheese has that Old World feel of perfection.

Preferes des Montagnes from the Jura Mountains is a wonderful option if Reblochon is unavailable. Both cheeses have edible bloom rinds and delicate nutty, buttery cow's milk flavors. And, yes, they melt like a dream!

Peel the potatoes and cut them into slices roughly ¼ in/6 mm thick.

Heat the olive oil in a large sauté pan. Sweat the onion over medium-low heat for about 10 minutes, or until translucent. Add the bacon and cook for about 5 minutes longer, until the onion is starting to gild and the bacon just begins to crisp. Drain a bit of the bacon fat from the pan but leave most of it for the potatoes.

Add the potatoes and toss to coat well with the onion, bacon, and residual bacon fat. Sauté for a few more minutes over medium-high heat. Season with salt and pepper. Add the wine, cover the pan, and reduce the heat to low. Simmer for 10 minutes.

Preheat the oven to 475°F/240C°/gas 9.

Rub the inside of a ceramic gratin dish with the garlic and then grease with the duck fat.

Add the crème fraîche to the potatoes, stir to combine, and then pour the mixture into the prepared gratin dish. Cut the half wheel of cheese in half again. Place the two pieces on top of the potatoes.

Bake in the center of the oven for about 20 minutes, or until the cheese is melted, bubbly, and golden.

Remove the tartiflette from the oven and let stand for 5 minutes before serving.

TARTIFLETTE

SERVES 6

3 lb/1.4 kg waxy yellow potatoes such as Yukon gold

2 tbsp olive oil

1 medium onion, chopped

6 oz/170 g smoked bacon, chopped

Salt and freshly cracked black pepper

½ cup/120 ml dry white wine

1 garlic clove, peeled

2 tbsp duck fat or unsalted butter

⅓ cup/75 ml crème fraîche

½ wheel (8 oz/225 g) Reblochon de Savoie or Preferes des Montagnes cheese

Potatoes and truffles are a match made in heaven. This dish is a bit like a Spanish tortilla and is a fantastic accompaniment to roasted fowl or grilled/barbecued steaks. It also can be served as a delicious and hearty dish for lunch with a radicchio salad or bitter greens, which contrast beautifully with the richness of the fried potatoes and melted cheese.

POTATO GRATIN WITH BLACK TRUFFLE CHEESE AND FRESH THYME

SERVES 4

1 lb/455 g russet potatoes

Flour, for dredging

2 eggs

8 tbsp/110 g unsalted butter

2 tbsp extra-virgin olive oil

Salt and freshly cracked black pepper

1 lb/455 g Sottocenere cheese, cut into thin slices

2 tsp fresh thyme, roughly chopped

Add the potatoes to a large pot of well-salted cold water over high heat. Bring to a boil, and then turn down the heat and simmer for 15 to 20 minutes, or until the potatoes are easily pierced with a knife. Drain, peel, and let cool slightly. Cut the cooked potatoes into slices about ⅛ in/3 mm thick.

Add the flour to a medium bowl. Add the eggs to a second bowl and beat them lightly.

Heat 4 tbsp/55 g of the butter along with the olive oil in a large frying pan. Dredge the potatoes in the flour and then dip in the beaten eggs and fry for 2 to 3 minutes, or until golden on both sides. Drain on paper towels and season with salt and pepper.

Preheat the oven to 375°F/190°C/gas 6.

Butter an 8-in/20-cm oval or round baking dish. Place some of the fried potatoes in a single layer in the prepared dish. Top with slices of cheese and some of the thyme. Continue with another layer of potatoes, and so forth, ending with a final layer of cheese and thyme. Dot the top with the remaining butter. Season with salt and pepper.

Bake on the middle rack of the oven for 20 minutes, or until golden brown. Let stand for 10 minutes. Serve hot or at room temperature.

Cypress Grove Dairy in Arcata, California, may be best known for its revolutionary cheese, Humboldt Fog, but these cheese makers have a few other tricks up their sleeves as well. Following a Dutch Gouda recipe, Midnight Moon is made in Holland for Cypress Grove using 100 percent goat milk. It is aged a minimum of six months and has a buttery, caramel flavor to it. When melted, the "goat comes out of the barn" and the aroma is divine for those of us who are goat cheese fiends.

Preheat the oven to 400°F/200°C/gas 6.

Wash the potatoes and dry them with a kitchen towel. Poke each potato with a fork in several places to allow steam to escape and to prevent the potatoes from exploding. Rub the potatoes all over with the olive oil and place directly on the middle or top rack of the oven. Bake for 1 hour and 15 minutes, or until the potatoes are tender throughout.

Allow the potatoes to cool enough to handle. Cut the potatoes in half lengthwise. Using a soupspoon, scoop out the insides, leaving about ¼ in/6 mm of potato flesh around the skin. Eat or discard the skin from one potato, as the flesh of one potato will provide the mash to help fill the other skins.

Place the insides of the potatoes in a medium bowl. Add the sour cream, milk, butter, cream, cheese, and chives. Mix with a fork or potato masher until well combined; do not overmix, or the potatoes will become gluey.

Spoon the mashed potatoes into the potato shells. The potatoes can be prepared to this point up to a day ahead, kept in the refrigerator, and returned to room temperature before proceeding.

Preheat the oven to 350°F/180°C/gas 4.

Place the filled potato skins on a baking sheet/tray and bake for 15 to 20 minutes, or until heated through. Serve hot.

TWICE-BAKED POTATOES WITH MIDNIGHT MOON GOAT CHEESE

MAKES 8 POTATO HALVES

5 large russet potatoes

2 tbsp extra-virgin olive oil

½ cup/120 ml sour cream

½ cup/120 ml whole milk

2 tbsp unsalted butter, at room temperature

1 tbsp heavy/double cream

1 cup/115 g grated Midnight Moon or other aged goat's milk Gouda cheese

¼ cup/15 g minced fresh chives

ASPARAGUS AND POTATO FRITTERS WITH MANOURI CHEESE, CHILIES, AND MINT

MAKES 24 FRITTERS

1 lb/455 g asparagus

4 oz/115 g Manouri cheese

½ cup/50 g grated Pecorino Romano cheese

1 medium Yukon gold potato, boiled and mashed

1 egg, beaten

2 tbsp bread crumbs

1 tbsp chopped fresh mint

1 tsp crushed dried red chilies

1 tbsp all-purpose/plain flour

Freshly cracked black pepper

Canola or grapeseed oil, for frying

Manouri is a fresh, beautifully white cheese made from the drained whey of feta production in Greece. Mainly sheep's milk, it is similar in flavor to traditional feta, but is far creamier and less salty.

Trim the asparagus of any woody ends. Bring a large pot of salted water to a boil. Blanch the asparagus for 3 to 5 minutes, depending on the size, until cooked but still firm.

Shock the asparagus in a bowl of ice water and then quickly remove and drain well. Pat dry and set out for a few minutes to dry further. Cut the cooked asparagus into medium dice and place in a medium mixing bowl. Add both cheeses, the mashed potato, egg, bread crumbs, mint, chilies, flour, and a few grindings of pepper. Mix well and refrigerate for at least 20 minutes.

Heat about 2 cups/480 ml canola oil in a large, shallow frying pan until hot but not smoking. Form the asparagus batter into small walnut-size balls and fry in the oil for 2 to 3 minutes, or until deep golden brown. Drain well on brown paper bags or paper towels. Serve hot or at room temperature.

When people tell me they don't like goat cheese, I love to give them a sample of goat's milk Gouda. Invariably they are shocked to learn that not all goat cheese is, well, "goaty." A young goat Gouda can be tangy, creamy, and nutty. It is ideal for sandwiches, especially with a few paper-thin slices of mortadella with pistachios. It is also a great melting cheese, though, when heated, the "goatiness" is a bit more pronounced.

Wash and dry the zucchini/courgettes. Cut off the stems and grate the vegetables with a cheese grater.

Place the grated zucchini/courgettes in a clean kitchen towel and squeeze out as much liquid as possible.

Transfer to a mixing bowl and add the shallot, cheese, flour, baking powder, salt, parsley, and a few grindings of pepper. Add the egg and bread crumbs, mixing well.

Heat the olive oil in a large, shallow frying pan over medium-high heat until hot but not smoking. Using a tablespoon, drop the batter into the hot oil and flatten with the side of the spoon to form round fritters. Cook for a minute or two and then flip and cook for another minute until both sides are deep golden brown.

Drain well on brown paper shopping bags or paper towels.

The fritters can be served hot, warm, or at room temperature. They are best when made and eaten in the same day, but they do refrigerate well. Reheat in a hot oven for 10 to 12 minutes, until heated through, and serve.

ZUCCHINI AND GOAT GOUDA FRITTERS

SERVES 4

2 medium zucchini/courgettes

1 large shallot, chopped fine

2 oz/55 g goat's milk Gouda cheese, grated

½ cup/60 g all-purpose/plain flour

¼ tsp baking powder

¼ tsp salt

3 tbsp chopped fresh flat-leaf parsley

Freshly cracked black pepper

1 egg

¼ cup/30 g bread crumbs

1 cup/240 ml olive oil, for frying

FRIED ZUCCHINI BLOSSOMS WITH TOMME DE MA GRANDE-MÈRE AND CITRUS HONEY

MAKES 12 BLOSSOMS

FOR THE BLOSSOMS

12 very fresh zucchini/courgette blossoms

12 oz/360 g Tomme de Ma Grande-mère or other young fresh goat cheese

FOR THE BATTER

1 egg

1 cup/240 ml ice water, plus more if needed

1 cup/125 g all-purpose/plain flour

2 cups/480 ml canola or grapeseed oil, for frying

Citrus flower honey, for dipping

Tomme de Ma Grande-mère, "cheese as grand-mother makes it," is a mild bloom rind goat cheese made just south of France's Loire Valley. Great in the summer with light fare and cool wines, the delicate paste has a rich mushroom-like flavor that appears just after the initial tangy kick of a great goat cheese. It is a lovely balance to the crispy fried texture of zucchini/courgette flowers. The honey brings it all together most elegantly.

TO PREPARE THE BLOSSOMS: Brush the zucchini/courgette blossoms with a pastry brush to remove any sand. Gently reach inside each one with the tips of your fingers and remove the pistil, being careful not to tear the flower. Stuff each blossom with 1 oz/30 g of the cheese. Twist the flowers closed at the ends.

TO PREPARE THE BATTER: In a medium bowl, whisk the egg with the ice water. Add the flour and whisk until smooth. Add more ice cold water if necessary to form a thick batter similar to crêpe batter. Refrigerate until ready to use.

Heat the canola oil to 350°F/180°C over medium heat. Dip the stuffed blossoms in the batter two or three at a time, and fry for about 2 minutes, or until light golden brown and crisp. Drain on paper towels and serve with the honey.

ROASTED BUTTERNUT SQUASH WITH FRESH TUSCAN PECORINO AND DEVIL'S HONEY

SERVES 4 TO 6

This recipe comes from my friend Brooke Burton; she had been served a similar dish on her honeymoon in Italy and wanted to re-create it at home. We set out together to find the perfect cheese to use, as she wasn't given the recipe (sneaky cook!).

As she described the dish, the flavors and textures seemed indelibly planted in her heart so it didn't take much experimenting. Turns out the cheese was a fresh Tuscan Pecorino, and although a mozzarella or even a Jack would work, there is something about combining the tang of sheep's milk and the creaminess of the squash that just works perfectly. The chili-spiked wildflower honey is my own addition, as the sweet heat cuts through the richness of this fantastic dish.

cont'd

FOR THE SQUASH
2 butternut squash

6 tbsp/90 ml extra-virgin olive oil

Sea salt

½ lb/225 g fresh pecorino cheese,
cut into ¼-in-/6-mm-thick squared slices

FOR THE DEVIL'S HONEY
½ cup/120 ml wildflower honey

¼ tsp crushed red chilies

TO PREPARE THE SQUASH: Preheat the oven to 375°F/
190°C/gas 5.

Peel the squash and cut the neck of each squash into
1-in/2.5-cm rounds. Reserve the bottoms of the squash for
another use. Drizzle with a little olive oil. Use your fingers
to coat every side of the squash rounds with the oil. Season
with sea salt.

Bake the squash rounds on a baking sheet/tray for
20 to 30 minutes, or until the squash is tender to the touch
of a fork. Set aside until cool enough to handle.

Lightly oil a baking dish and either layer the slices of
cooked squash and cheese *au cheval* (shingled like fallen
dominoes) or stack up in towers. Bake for 15 to 20 minutes,
or until the cheese is runny and gooey.

TO PREPARE THE DEVIL'S HONEY: Combine the honey and
chilies in a small saucepan. Cook gently over medium heat until
the honey just begins to bubble. Remove from the heat and
let cool to room temperature.

Drizzle the honey over the squash before serving.

Pecorino Piacentinu is a sheep's milk cheese spiked with wild saffron and studded with whole black peppercorns. It is made in the ancient city of Enna in central Sicily, using very traditional methods. The 9-lb/4-kg wheels are magnificent, bearing the marks of the wicker baskets in which they are aged. It is a fairly salty yet mild-flavored table cheese, until one bites into the whole peppercorns. When the cheese melts, the aroma of saffron kicks in. I omit the use of salt and pepper in the final baking, as the cheese does the trick for both.

Using a small sharp paring knife, trim the broccolini of its tough outer membrane starting with the base and peeling up toward the florets. Bring plenty of salted water to a boil in a large pot. Add the trimmed broccolini and cook for 4 to 5 minutes, or until just cooked but still very firm. Drain and lay the broccolini out flat to help them cool down and prevent them from overcooking.

In a large frying pan, heat 2 tbsp of the olive oil until hot but not smoking. Add the shallots and sauté over medium heat for 3 to 5 minutes, or until deeply caramelized and crisp. Remove from the heat and set aside.

Preheat the oven to 400°F/200°C/gas 6.

Grease a large gratin dish or baking sheet/tray with 2 tbsp of the oil. Lay the cooked and cooled broccolini in the pan and scatter the crispy shallots on top. Sprinkle with the grated cheese and then the bread crumbs. Finally, drizzle the remaining olive oil over the top.

Bake for 20 to 25 minutes, or until the surface is golden and crisp. Remove from the oven and serve.

BROCCOLINI WITH CARAMELIZED SHALLOTS AND SICILIAN PECORINO WITH SAFFRON

SERVES 8

2 lb/910 g broccolini

6 tbsp/60 ml extra-virgin olive oil

4 large shallots, sliced

2½ oz/70 g Pecorino Piacentinu cheese, grated

½ cup/60 g bread crumbs

I love Greek feta. I love Bulgarian feta. And I could not live without French feta. A fairly recent creation, French feta comes from the south of France and is creamier, milder, and far less salty than its Eastern cousins. In my refrigerator at home, I keep a piece of French feta with a good amount of the brine in which it is cured.

French feta—whether cut into chunks and tossed with butter/Boston lettuce, grapefruit, and thin slices of red onion or crumbled over cucumbers, cherry tomatoes, a splash of extra-virgin olive oil, and loads of fresh basil—is a great rescue for last-minute lunch dilemmas. It is also divine warm and blends beautifully with eggplant/aubergine.

Heat a large frying pan or flat-top griddle over medium heat. Add a bit of the olive oil to coat the bottom of the pan and then add the eggplant/aubergine in small batches. Sauté for 12 to 15 minutes, or until golden brown, seasoning well with salt and pepper.

Add a bit of oil as needed, but remember that the eggplant/aubergine will take what you give it and keep asking for more.

Transfer the cooked eggplant/aubergine to a warm serving dish. Crumble the feta and basil over the eggplant/aubergine.

Fry the bread pieces in the remaining oil for about 3 minutes, or until crispy and golden. Scatter the croutons over the eggplant/aubergine and serve hot or at room temperature.

GOLDEN EGGPLANT WITH CREAMY FRENCH FETA AND CROUTONS

SERVES 4 TO 6

8 to 10 tbsp/120 to 150 ml extra-virgin olive oil

2 large eggplants/aubergines, cut into ¾-in/2-cm dice

Salt and freshly cracked black pepper

½ lb/225 g French feta cheese

¼ cup/15 g roughly chopped fresh basil

1 cup/60 g day-old French bread, cut or torn into ¾-in/2-cm pieces

This could almost be considered a grilled salad, as the radicchio wedges, though charred on the outside, remain very much raw internally. The crispy pancetta and melted smoky provolone wrap themselves around the bitter bite of the radicchio in a heavenly way. Grilled radicchio can be served as a *contorno*, or side dish, to grilled or roasted meats, and it is particularly divine alongside fish.

Cut the radicchio into four wedges. Place a slice of the cheese on each piece and then wrap a slice of pancetta around it as well.

Heat a gas grill/barbecue to high heat or build a hot fire in a charcoal grill/barbecue. Drizzle the wrapped radicchio wedges with the olive oil and place them on the grill/barbecue. Cook for 3 to 5 minutes, or until the pancetta is crisp on one side, and then turn with tongs to crisp the remaining edges. The cheese should melt nicely during this process, but if the pancetta is crisp and golden before the cheese has completely melted, simply place the radicchio wedges in a 400°F/200°C/gas 6 oven for a few more minutes. Serve hot or at room temperature.

GRILLED RADICCHIO WITH SMOKED PROVOLONE AND PANCETTA

SERVES 4

1 head radicchio

4 thin slices smoked Caciocavallo or mozzarella cheese

4 thin slices pancetta

1 tbsp extra-virgin olive oil

CRACKERS, FLATBREADS, AND PIZZA

Bread and cheese—the humble meal of monks and shepherds. Volumes could be written on the many ways crackers, breads, and pizza are indelibly connected to cheese. Local artisan bread makers and gourmet cheese shops brimming with biscuits and crackers offer everything you may need to serve cheese on, except the pride of making these items yourself.

I remember visiting the village wood-burning bread oven in San Ciperello just outside Palermo, Italy, where the local mamas and *nonnas* would bring their dough down to make bread for the week. While massive loaves were formed and left to rest, the wise ladies would pinch off balls of dough the size of their hands, flatten them like tortillas, and toss them onto the blackened floor of the roaring brick oven. In a matter of minutes, the dough would puff up like oversized Ping-Pong balls. The rolls were taken out, cut in half immediately (so much for the rule about not eating bread while it's still hot), drowned in home-pressed extra-virgin olive oil, and sprinkled with red chilies and the shavings of salty Caciocavallo cheese.

Not all of us have wood-burning ovens like the old villages of Europe (or the trendy restaurants down the street!), but when it comes to pizza and focaccia, we have tools at our disposal and cheeses available that will help bring some of those Old World flavors back home.

The spicy kick in these little bites is perfectly balanced with a deep, rich Cheddar flavor. My dear friend Dean insists on calling them "Jeez-its" because, he says, "Christ, they're good!"

The key to these diamonds is to use the very best aged Cheddar possible. Montgomery's Cheddar from Neal's Yard Dairy in London is a good barometer of quality, although in the United States some amazing bandage-wrapped Cheddars are being produced, notably Flagship Cheddar from Beecher's in Seattle.

In a bowl, whisk together the flour, salt, and chilies. Transfer to the bowl of a food processor fitted with the blade attachment. Add the butter and pulse until the mixture resembles coarse meal. Add the cheese and pulse to combine.

Add 3 tablespoons of the water, a tablespoon at a time, pulsing until the mixture comes together in a ball. Pulse in an additional tablespoon of water if needed to get the dough to hold together. Wrap the dough in plastic wrap/cling film and chill for at least an hour.

Preheat the oven to 350°F/180°C/gas 4.

Roll the dough out to a ⅛-in/3-mm thickness directly onto a baking sheet/tray. This thickness should be accurate, as the diamonds will not puff up nicely if the dough is too thin, nor will they be crispy enough if the dough is too thick.

Cut the dough into ½-in/12-mm diamonds (or whichever shape you prefer) using a cookie cutter, sharp knife, or fluted pasta cutter. Spread out the cut pieces onto three parchment/baking paper–lined baking sheets/trays, giving them just enough room so that they are not touching. Bake for 35 to 40 minutes, or until the crackers are deep golden brown and crunchy. Let cool completely before serving. The diamonds can be stored in an airtight container for up to 1 week, although they are best the first couple of days.

RED CHILI AND CHEDDAR DIAMONDS

MAKES ABOUT 180 CRACKERS

1 cup/125 g all-purpose/plain flour

¾ tsp salt

1 tsp crushed red chilies

4 tbsp/56 g unsalted butter, chilled and diced

8 oz/225 g best-quality aged Cheddar cheese, grated

3 to 4 tbsp water

WINE: Any whites, reds, rosés
OTHER: Beer, cocktails, just about anything potable!

MAYTAG MADELEINES WITH WILDFLOWER HONEY

MAKES 24 MADELEINES

7 tbsp/100 g unsalted butter, plus extra for greasing

3½ oz/100 g Maytag Blue, Saint Agur, or other soft blue cheese

3 eggs

1 cup plus 2 tbsp/130 g all-purpose/plain flour

2 tsp baking powder

A pinch of salt

Freshly cracked black pepper

Wildflower honey for drizzling

My son loves madeleines. Buttery and sweet, they are that simple kind of cake that makes a perfect after-school snack. His enthusiasm for them poured over to his mother and me to the extent that our newborn daughter landed with the middle name Madeleine.

This recipe for savory madeleines, inspired by Clotilde Dusoulier's version in *Chocolate & Zucchini*, is not to the taste of this cheesemonger's son, but they are a delight for those of us who love blue cheese and are constantly looking for new ways to enjoy it.

Preheat the oven to 400°F/200°C/gas 6. Grease a madeleine mold with butter.

Combine the butter and blue cheese in the bowl of an electric mixer fitted with the paddle attachment. Cream together until smooth and well combined. Slowly add the eggs, one at a time, incorporating well between additions. In a separate bowl, sift together the flour, baking powder, salt, and a few grindings of pepper. Add the dry ingredients to the butter, egg, and cheese mixture.

Add a heaping teaspoon of the batter into each mold, filling each almost to the rim.

Bake for 15 minutes, or until lightly golden brown. Let cool completely before serving with a drizzle of wildflower honey.

WINE: Sweet dessert wines such as Rivesaltes Ambré, Vin Santo

Although there is a massive variety of delicious crackers and cheese biscuits available in the markets, the idea of having something homemade to enjoy with cheese just makes sense to me, at least when time permits.

The simplicity of these crackers is actually their biggest attribute. Having said so, feel free to experiment with fresh herbs such as rosemary, fruits such as dried apricots, chopped olives, or nuts to add in small amounts to this dough.

Preheat the oven to 350°F/180°C/gas 4.

Mix the flour, salt, and baking powder in a large bowl. Add the olive oil and water and mix well. The dough will be a little sticky, but it shouldn't be hard to handle. If it feels too sticky, add a little more flour.

Roll out the dough on a well-floured work surface to 1/16 in/2 mm. This is where a pasta machine comes in handy; it will not only give you the thin sheets you're looking for but it will also give your batch of crackers a more uniform look, should you care about such things.

Lower the oven racks to the bottom half of the oven, to ensure more even cooking. Cut the dough into squares, rectangles, or whatever cracker shapes you like. Lightly grease two baking sheets/trays and place the crackers on them about 1/2 in/12 mm apart. Prick the crackers with a fork to prevent them from puffing up too much; this will also give them the classic "Saltines" look.

Bake for 15 to 20 minutes, or until crisp and lightly golden.

Let cool completely before serving. The crackers can be stored in an airtight container for several weeks.

SEA-SALTINE CRACKERS

MAKES ABOUT 50 CRACKERS

1¼ cups/155 g all-purpose/plain flour, plus extra if needed

½ tsp coarse sea salt

¼ tsp baking powder

1½ tbsp extra-virgin olive oil, plus extra for greasing

½ cup/120 ml warm water

WINE: Make your wine selection based on the cheese you are serving.

More like two sheets of paper-thin crackers sand-wiching one the greatest soft cheeses of all time, fresh stracchino, this is not the typical Italian olive-oil bread.

Crescenza is a good version of the stracchino cheese, with a texture like ripe Taleggio and a sweet buttermilk tang. This is one of those dishes best made with friends standing nearby, as it should be devoured straight from the oven. Those of you with wood-burning ovens that can reach higher temperatures are in for a treat!

In a large mixing bowl, combine the flour, water, and 3 tbsp of the olive oil. Knead by hand until a smooth and elastic dough is formed. Shape the dough into a ball, set it back into the bowl, and cover it with a kitchen towel. Allow the dough to rest for at least 1 hour.

Preheat the oven to 500°F/260°C/gas 10.

When the dough is rested, divide it into two pieces. Roll out each piece separately on a lightly floured surface until the dough is paper thin, so that the color of your hand can be seen through it. The masters work the dough like a traditional pizza, using the knuckles of both hands to move the dough in circles off the table. Alternatively, you can use a pasta machine to make rectangle versions, which is actually quite practical for parties.

Grease a round pizza tray 20 in/50 cm in diameter (or rectangular baking sheet/tray) with 2 tbsp of the remaining olive oil. Place one sheet of dough on the pan.

cont'd

FOCACCIA DI RECCO— LIGURIAN CRACKER BREAD WITH STRACCHINO

MAKES ONE 20-IN/50-CM FOCACCIA

2½ cups/315 g all-purpose/plain flour

¾ cup/180 ml tepid water

½ cup/120 ml extra-virgin olive oil

8 oz/225 g stracchino or Crescenza cheese

Coarse sea salt for sprinkling

Tear the cheese into golf ball–size pieces and scatter evenly over the surface of the dough. Place the other sheet of dough on top and, using the palm of your hand, flatten slightly the mounds formed by the cheese. Gently rub the surface with the remaining olive oil and create a few holes in the top sheet of dough by pinching and tearing here and there. Sprinkle a bit of sea salt over the surface and bake for 15 to 20 minutes, or until crispy and golden, with a few burn spots being perfectly desirable and pools of melted cheese forming around the tears.

Cut into squares and serve immediately.

WHITE WINE: Pigato from Liguria
RED WINE: Aglianico

Unlike the Focaccia di Recco, this is a well-known olive-oil bread from Italy. Sottocenere al Tartufo is a raw cow's milk cheese from the Veneto region, laced with black truffles and coated with an exotic rub of ash, nutmeg, coriander, cinnamon, licorice, cloves, and fennel. *Sottocenere* literally translates as "under the ashes" and is a very popular table cheese. It also melts like a dream, with the perfume of truffle that is sublime with paper-thin slices of crisp potato.

Place the water in a large bowl. Sprinkle the yeast onto the surface of the water, along with the salt and sugar. Let stand for 5 minutes to dissolve and then add half of the flour. Stir to form a very wet and sticky starter dough. Place a kitchen towel over the bowl and let the dough stand at room temperature for 2 hours.

When the dough has rested and risen by about a third, add the remaining flour along with 1 tbsp of the olive oil. Stir to combine and then turn the dough out onto a lightly floured surface. Knead the dough for 5 to 10 minutes, or until it is sticky but has a spring to the touch. Place the dough back in the bowl, rub with a small amount of the olive oil, cover, and let rest for another hour.

Turn the dough out onto a lightly floured surface. Using the tips of your fingers and the palms of your hands, press and stretch out the dough to form a 12-by-16-in/30-by-40-cm rectangle. The dough will be quite springy, so let it rest a bit between stretching. Rub a 12-by-16-in/30-by-40-cm baking sheet/tray with 2 tbsp of the olive oil. Transfer the dough to the oiled pan and, using only your fingertips, push the dough to the borders of the pan, allowing your fingertips to form deep imprints. Lay the slices of Sottocenere over the top. Cover lightly with a kitchen towel and let rest for 30 minutes.

cont'd

FOCACCIA WITH VENETIAN BLACK TRUFFLE CHEESE AND POTATOES

MAKES ONE 12-BY-16-IN/
30-BY-40-CM FOCACCIA

1½ cups/360 ml lukewarm water

2¼ tsp active dry yeast

½ tsp salt

½ tsp sugar

3½ cups/440 g all-purpose/plain flour

6 tbsp/90 ml extra-virgin olive oil

3 oz/85 g Sottocenere al Tartufo cheese, sliced thin

1 large russet or Yukon gold potato

1 tbsp roughly chopped fresh sage leaves

Sea salt and freshly cracked black pepper

Preheat the oven to 400°F/200°C/gas 6.

When the dough is ready to bake, slice the potato paper-thin using a mandoline or very sharp knife. Doing this at the last minute will help prevent the potato from oxidizing. Lay slices of potato over the Sottocenere in an overlapping pattern that the French call *au cheval*, or horseback. Scatter the sage leaves over the potato slices and drizzle the remaining olive oil over the entire surface. Sprinkle with sea salt and pepper.

Bake for 25 to 30 minutes, or until the top is golden and the bottom is cooked through. This focaccia is best served slightly warm from the oven, but never serve it hot.

WHITE WINE: Friulano, Soave

FOCACCIA WITH BLACK OLIVES, PECORINO FRESCO DELL'AMIATA, AND ORANGE ZEST

MAKES ONE 12-BY-16-IN/
30-BY-40-CM FOCACCIA

1½ cups/360 ml lukewarm water

2¼ tsp active dry yeast

½ tsp salt

½ tsp sugar

3½ cups/440 g all-purpose/plain flour

6 tbsp/90 ml extra-virgin olive oil

½ cup/115 g black oil-cured olives,
pitted and roughly chopped

1 tbsp finely chopped fresh rosemary

3 oz/85 g fresh pecorino cheese, preferably
Pecorino Fresco dell'Amiata cheese,
sliced thin

Sea salt and freshly cracked black pepper
for sprinkling

2 large oranges, for zesting

Young sheep's milk cheeses can be found in a variety of forms from numerous regions of Italy, though the one I prefer for this delightfully simple focaccia comes from the mountain town of Amiata in Southern Tuscany's Maremma, where the wild Maremmano horses still roam and Tuscan cowboys called *butteri* still wrangle the great Chianina cattle for their prized steaks!

Ultra-creamy, sweet, and tangy, Pecorino Fresco dell'Amiata has a texture similar to Bel Paese, which lends itself well to melting. A young caciotta or fresh pecorino from Rome or Umbria and even a Primo Sale from Sicily would do nicely as well.

Proceed precisely as in the recipe for Focaccia with Venetian Black Truffle Cheese and Potatoes on page 119, adding the olives to the dough during the second addition of flour as you knead. After transferring the dough to the oiled baking sheet/tray, sprinkle the rosemary over the surface and then the slices of pecorino. Let rest for 30 minutes.

Sprinkle with sea salt and pepper, drizzle the remaining oil over the surface, and then grate the oranges directly on the cheese. Bake as directed in previous recipe. Cut into squares and serve warm or at room temperature.

RED WINE: Chianti Classico, Nero d'Avola, Châteauneuf-du-Pape, Bandol

PIZZA BIANCA WITH ROASTED MUSHROOMS AND FONTINA

MAKES THREE 11-BY-5-IN/
28-BY-12-CM PIZZAS

FOR THE DOUGH

1½ cups/360 ml lukewarm water

2¼ tsp active dry yeast

½ tsp salt

½ tsp sugar

3½ cups/440 g all-purpose/plain flour

4 tbsp/60 ml extra-virgin olive oil

In the colorful market square of Campo Di Fiori near the Piazza Navona in Rome, tucked away in the corner next to Trattoria La Carbonara, is the unbelievable mecca of Roman baked goods, humbly named Forno. Packed with locals and tourists alike, the small storefront offers a dizzying array of tempting breads typical of Rome. In the morning, steaming hot *maritozzi*—a sweet bun studded with candied orange peel, pine nuts, and raisins—can be had for a song, but later in the day comes the real treat: savory 8-ft-/2.5-m-long pizza, stacked on rungs and cut to the desires of the greedy customers!

TO PREPARE THE DOUGH: Place the water in a large bowl. Sprinkle the yeast onto the surface of the water, along with the salt and sugar. Let stand for 5 minutes to dissolve and then add half the flour. Stir to form a very wet and sticky starter dough. Place a kitchen towel over the bowl and let the dough stand at room temperature for 2 hours.

When the dough has rested and risen by about a third, add the remaining flour along with 3 tbsp of the olive oil. Stir to combine and then turn the dough out onto a lightly floured surface. Knead the dough for 5 to 10 minutes, or until it is sticky but has a spring to the touch. Divide the dough into three balls, place in separate bowls, and rub with the remaining olive oil. Cover and let rest for another hour.

Spread the mushrooms out on a baking sheet/tray and toss with 3 tbsp of the olive oil. Season well with salt and pepper. Roast the mushrooms for 10 to 12 minutes, or until tender and golden. Remove from the heat and set aside to cool.

In a small frying pan, combine ½ cup/120 ml of the olive oil with the garlic and cook over very low heat for 7 to 8 minutes, or until the garlic is soft and just slightly golden.

Remove the garlic from the oil and set aside to cool. The garlic-infused oil can be set aside and later used to dress a simple pasta or for dipping with good crusty bread and some fresh goat cheese.

Preheat the oven to 500°F/260°C/gas 10. Remove all racks and place an inverted 16-by-12 in/40.5-by-30.5-cm baking sheet/tray on the floor of the oven (most pizza stones are not long enough for this shape pizza).

Working with one ball at a time, turn the dough out onto a well-floured surface and, using your fingertips and palms of your hands, gently stretch each ball out into a rectangle about 11 by 5 in/28 by 12 cm.

Scatter a small amount of coarse cornmeal onto the inverted bottom of another 16-by-12-in/40.5-by-30.5-cm baking sheet/tray. (This will act as your pizza peel.)

Place the shaped dough onto the pan. Squeeze 3 of the garlic cloves with your fingertips and gently spread randomly over the dough. Scatter a third of the cooked mushrooms and follow with a third of the fontina. Season with salt and freshly cracked black pepper and then drizzle with 4 tbsp/60 ml of the olive oil.

Working quickly and carefully, open the oven door and shake the pizza onto the hot pan. If you are uncomfortable doing this, the pizza can be baked directly on the pan it was assembled on, but the crust won't be quite as crisp.

Cook the pizza for 10 to 12 minutes, or until it is cooked on the bottom and the cheese is melted and golden. Carefully remove the pan with oven gloves and shake the pizza onto a large cutting board. Proceed with the rest of the dough and ingredients. Serve the pizza as hot as you can!

WINE: A pizza like this goes with just about everything medium weight, reds or whites. Perhaps a Gavi di Gavi or a Dolcetto in keeping with the regional flavors.

3 cups/70 g mixed mushrooms (I prefer tree oyster, cremini/brown, and chanterelle when available)

1¼ cups/300 ml plus 3 tbsp extra-virgin olive oil

Salt and freshly cracked black pepper

9 garlic cloves, peeled

Coarse cornmeal

12 oz/340 g Fontina Valle d'Aosta cheese, trimmed of rind and diced

It is said that Michelangelo Buonarotti himself loved the famous Casciotta cheese from Urbino in the Marche of Southern Italy so much that he purchased property there to ensure he would always have a supply of it.

Casciotta d'Urbino is a nutty, buttery semi-soft cheese made up of 70 percent cow's milk and 30 percent sheep's milk. Aged for only twenty days, it has a sweet and mellow flavor that I love to eat as is or quickly melt on a pizza with a simple puree of arugula/rocket, olive oil, and Pecorino Romano. A fresh Tuscan or other young pecorino works wonderfully as well.

TO PREPARE THE DOUGH: Place the water in a large bowl. Sprinkle the yeast on the surface of the water, along with the salt and sugar. Let stand for 5 minutes to dissolve and then add half of the flour. Stir to form a very wet and sticky starter dough. Place a kitchen towel over the bowl and let stand at room temperature for 2 hours.

When the dough has rested and risen by about a third, add the remaining flour along with 3 tbsp of the olive oil. Stir to combine and then turn the dough out onto a lightly floured surface. Knead the dough for 5 to 10 minutes, or until it is sticky but has a spring to the touch. Divide the dough into twelve balls and place them next to each other on a baking sheet/tray greased with 1 tbsp of the oil. Rub the dough balls with the remaining olive oil. Cover and let rest for another hour.

TO PREPARE THE PESTO: Place the arugula/rocket and the pecorino in the bowl of a food processor fitted with the blade attachment. Puree, adding the olive oil in a steady stream until smooth, scraping down the sides of the bowl as needed.

cont'd

PIZZETTE WITH ARUGULA PESTO AND CASCIOTTA D'URBINO

MAKES 12 PIZZETTES

FOR THE DOUGH
1½ cups/360 ml lukewarm water

¼ oz/2.5 g active dry yeast

½ tsp salt

½ tsp sugar

3½ cups/440 g all-purpose/plain flour

5 tbsp/75 ml extra-virgin olive oil

FOR THE PESTO
3 cups/90 g (packed) wild arugula/rocket leaves

¼ cup/25 g freshly grated Pecorino Romano cheese

¼ cup/60 ml extra-virgin olive oil

FOR THE PIZZETTE
Coarse cornmeal

2 cups/340 g toy box or cherry tomatoes, halved

18 oz/510 g Casciotta d'Urbino or fresh pecorino cheese, sliced ⅟₁₆ in/2 mm thick

Crushed red chilies

TO ASSEMBLE THE PIZZETTE: Preheat the oven to 500°F/ 260°C/gas 10. Remove all racks and place a pizza stone or inverted 16-by-12-in/40.5-by-30.5-cm baking sheet/tray on the oven floor.

Working with one ball at a time, turn the dough out onto a well-floured surface and, using your fingertips and palms of your hands, gently stretch each ball out into a circle 6 in/15 cm in diameter. Scatter a small amount of coarse cornmeal onto a pizza peel or baking sheet/tray with no sides before placing a dough round on it. Spread 1 tbsp of the pesto on the dough and top with 2 oz/55g of the tomatoes and 1½ oz/40 g of the Casciotta d'Urbino cheese. Add a pinch of red chilies. Open the oven door and shake the pizza onto the preheated pizza stone or baking sheet/ tray. Cook for 5 to 7 minutes, until the bottom of the pizza is crisp and golden. Remove with a pizza peel or inverted spatula, taking care not to get burned. Proceed with the remaining dough and ingredients. Serve immediately.

WHITE WINE: Orvieto

Yorkshire puddings, or popovers as they are known in the United States, are an absolute must for my Christmas dinner, and I am a bit of a purist on that day about the classic accompaniment to roasted beef. But I am all for experimenting with the classics, and I have discovered that while a plain pudding suits the roasted beef of winter, these light and airy parmesan-scented puddings are delightful with a roasted pork loin or chicken the rest of the year.

In a medium bowl, whisk together the flour and yeast. Stir in the fromage blanc, eggs, olive oil, Parmigiano, and salt. Let the batter rest for at least 30 minutes.

Preheat the oven to 350°F/180°C/gas 4.

Distribute the batter equally in a 12-cup muffin pan/tin and bake for 30 minutes, or until the popovers are puffed and deep golden brown. Remove from the oven, turn the popovers out from the pan, and serve hot.

. . . .

RED WINE: Sangiovese, Tempranillo, Cabernet Franc, Côte du Rhone

PARMIGIANO POPOVERS

MAKES 12 POPOVERS

2 cups/255 g all-purpose/plain flour

2 tsp active dry yeast

10½ oz/300 g fromage blanc

3 eggs, beaten

2 tbsp extra-virgin olive oil

2 oz/55 g Parmigiano-Reggiano cheese, grated

⅛ tsp salt

ARTICHOKE FRITTATA WITH FRESH MOZZARELLA AND BASIL / 133

SAVORY CUPCAKES WITH PETIT BASQUE AND CHERRIES / 134

CALIFORNIA RAREBIT / 136

CHICKPEA FRITTERS WITH PRIMO SALE AND CHILIES / 137

BRIE DE MEAUX AND ROASTED FENNEL SANDWICH / 141

CLUB SANDWICH WITH GRAVLAX, AVOCADO, BACON, AND BEAUFORT / 143

MELTED FROMAGER D'AFFINOIS AND MADRANGE HAM SANDWICHES / 144

FRESH RICOTTA TORTA WITH WILD SPRING ONIONS / 146

ZUCCHINI AND CAMEMBERT TART / 149

FLAMICHE—BELGIAN TART WITH BACON, BEER, AND MUNSTER / 152

TARTS AND SANDWICHES

I recall reading that the tables at court of fourteenth-century Italy became so decadent that Sumptuary Laws were imposed, limiting the number of courses a meal could include. To get around these laws, pasticcio, or "savory pies," were invented to house a dizzying list of ingredients; the idea was that anything that could be crammed between two crusts would be considered a pie and, therefore, only one course!

The following recipes for tortas are far less opulent than those of the early Renaissance, I can assure you, but are nonetheless great ways to experience great cheeses.

Sandwiches, like soups, often defy the idea of a recipe as they are influenced by their surroundings. Great bread, amazing cheese, and perhaps a slice or two of cured pork is all it takes. Being surrounded by piles of fresh bread and mountains of glorious cheese, I am constantly toying with new combinations and have included a few of my favorites here.

Artichokes and eggs—the textures, the flavors, and the beautiful pastel palette of green and yellow sings of springtime when this dish should be made. It is wonderful when made in advance, cut into squares, and then either served cold or cooked on a flat-top griddle.

Fill a large pot with cold water. Squeeze the lemon into the water to acidulate it. (This will help prevent the artichokes from oxidizing.)

Leaving the stems on the artichokes, cut the sharp tips off the leaves with a pair of kitchen shears or a serrated bread knife and then submerge the artichokes in the water. Bring the water to a boil, reduce to a simmer, and then boil for 20 minutes, or until a knife inserted into the bottom center of an artichoke goes in easily. Drain and allow to cool.

Remove most of the outer tough leaves (saving them for an afternoon snack with some extra-virgin olive oil and sea salt). Peel and trim the stems and cut away the bristly choke. Cut each artichoke into eight pieces.

Preheat the oven to 400°F/200°C/gas 6.

In a medium bowl, whisk the eggs with the Parmigiano and season with salt and pepper. Line a 9-by-9-in/23-by-23-cm baking dish with parchment/baking paper and then grease with the olive oil.

Lay the artichokes in the bottom of the dish and scatter the mozzarella on top, followed by another layer of artichokes, mozzarella, and finally a top layer of artichokes. Sprinkle with the basil. Pour in the egg and Parmigiano mixture and move the dish about to evenly distribute the eggs.

Bake for 25 to 30 minutes, or until set and golden.

Serve at room temperature, cold, or toasted on a lightly buttered griddle.

WHITE WINE: Prosecco

ARTICHOKE FRITTATA WITH FRESH MOZZARELLA AND BASIL

SERVES 3 OR 4

½ lemon

8 small artichokes

6 eggs

3 oz/85 g grated Parmigiano-Reggiano cheese

Salt and freshly cracked black pepper

1 tbsp extra-virgin olive oil

7 oz/200 g fresh water buffalo's milk or cow's milk mozzarella cheese, cut into ¼-in/6-mm slices

½ cup/30 g chopped fresh basil

SAVORY CUPCAKES WITH PETIT BASQUE AND CHERRIES

MAKES 6 CUPCAKES

2 cups/255 g all-purpose/plain flour

1 tsp baking powder

Salt and freshly cracked black pepper

2 eggs

¾ cup/180 ml whole milk

½ cup/120 ml extra-virgin olive oil

8 oz/225 g Petit Basque or other mild Pyrenees sheep's milk cheese, grated

3½ oz/100 g fresh cherries, pitted and roughly chopped

⅔ cup/75 g pine nuts, toasted

There is a fantastic trend in France of making savory loaf breads, which they refer to as "cakes." Fillings and flavoring possibilities are endless, including fresh herbs, great cheese, and choice pieces of charcuterie. Often used to start a meal, these cupcakes can be the main course along with a salad, and are ideal for summer picnics and light spring lunches.

Petit Basque is a nutty, mild sheep's milk cheese from the French Pyrenees that has become readily available in cheese shops and better food stores. The list of wonderful Basque sheep's milk cheeses that could be substituted is endless, including Ossau-Iraty or Abbaye de Belloc, which is still made by Benedictine monks from milk often given in votive from local shepherds.

In the bowl of an electric mixer fitted with the paddle attachment, combine the flour, baking powder, ½ tsp salt, and a few grindings of pepper.

In a separate bowl, whisk together the eggs and milk and then add the olive oil. Turn the machine on to medium and add the wet mixture to the dry ingredients. Continue mixing until a sticky dough forms. Add the cheese, cherries, and pine nuts all at once and mix until the ingredients are just combined. Remove the bowl and paddle from the machine and cover the dough with a kitchen towel. Let rest for 30 minutes.

Preheat the oven to 400°F/200°C/gas 6. Place paper liners in six cups of a muffin pan/tin.

Divide the dough among the paper-lined cups. Bake for 20 minutes, or until golden and a wooden skewer inserted into the center of a cake comes out clean.

Let cool completely before serving.

WINE: Bugey, Dolcetto, and Côtes du Rhone wines, including rosé

CALIFORNIA RAREBIT

SERVES 4

¼ cup/60 ml whole milk

½ cup/60 g all-purpose/plain flour

14 oz/400 g grated Fiscalini Cheddar or other mature raw–cow's milk Cheddar cheese

1½ cups/170 g fresh bread crumbs

1 tsp dry English mustard powder

1 tbsp Worcestershire sauce

½ cup/120 ml Anchor Steam beer

Salt

1 egg, plus 1 egg yolk

1 sourdough baguette

This take on the classic Welsh rarebit utilizes two Northern Californian powerhouse ingredients, though any great Cheddar and good beer would work.

Fiscalini Farmstead Cheese in Modesto, California, makes one of the best raw-milk, bandage-wrapped cheddars that I've ever tasted. It is fantastic on its own but is a dream come true when melted. Our friends up the street at The Golden State restaurant here in Los Angeles make a cheeseburger with this Cheddar exclusively, and there is little wonder why.

In a heavy saucepan over medium heat, gently bring the milk to a simmer. Add the flour and bring to a boil, stirring constantly until the sauce begins to thicken, about 5 minutes. Remove from the heat, add the cheese, and then return to the heat and stir constantly until the cheese is melted. Add the bread crumbs, mustard powder, Worcestershire sauce, and beer. Season with salt. Continue cooking over low heat for about 3 minutes, or until the mixture just starts to separate from the side of the pan, somewhat like a choux pastry.

Take the pan off the heat and let cool to room temperature.

Place the mixture in the bowl of a food processor fitted with the blade attachment. Add the egg and egg yolk. Mix until blended and smooth. This mixture can be kept for several days if wrapped tightly and refrigerated.

Slice the baguette in half lengthwise and set the halves cut-sides up on a baking sheet/tray. Spread the cheese mixture over the surfaces of the bread and broil/grill until golden brown.

Cut each baguette half into four pieces and serve immediately.

RED WINE: Salice Salentino or Loire reds such as Bourgueil and Chinon
OTHER: your favorite beer

Walk through the narrow corridors of the Vuccira market in Palermo, Sicily, and amid the piles of vibrant produce, coils of offal, and tables crowded with well-armed but decapitated swordfish, you will find the *fritterie*, or fritter stands. There among all things fried and yummy are the *panelle*. Like a polenta made of chickpea flour, panelle are fried to order in vats of oil right in the street, and they are generally served unadorned, wrapped in paper or shoved into a sesame-seeded bun.

Primo Sale is literally the first salting of the spring's young sheep's milk cheeses; it can be found plain or studded with pistachios, walnuts, and even wild arugula/rocket. A young Tuscan or Umbrian pecorino will also do nicely for this recipe, as well as young Pyrenees Brebis such as Petit Basque or Abbaye de Belloc.

Combine the water, salt, and extra-virgin olive oil in a small saucepan. Place over medium heat and whisk in the flour, stirring constantly as the batter thickens.

Continue cooking for 15 to 20 minutes, whisking frequently, until the paste begins to pull away from the sides of the pan. Toss in the parsley and stir to combine.

Splash an 11-by-16-in/28-by-40.5-cm baking sheet/tray with cold water and then shake off the water, leaving the pan slightly wet. Pour the chickpea batter into the wet pan, spreading it evenly with a wet rubber spatula until it fills the pan in a smooth and even layer.

Refrigerate for at least 1 hour, or until firmly set. Then, with a sharp knife, cut the batter into rectangles about 2 by 3 in/5 by 7.5 cm.

cont'd

CHICKPEA FRITTERS WITH PRIMO SALE AND CHILIES

MAKES 10 TO 12 FRITTERS

2 cups/480 ml water

1 tsp coarse sea salt, plus more for sprinkling

¼ cup/60 ml extra-virgin olive oil

1¼ cups/115 g chickpea flour

¼ cup/15 g roughly chopped fresh flat-leaf parsley

½ cup/120 ml pure olive oil for frying

8 oz/225 g Primo Sale or other fresh pecorino cheese, thinly sliced

Crushed red chilies

Heat the pure olive oil in a shallow frying pan to 350°F/180°C. Fry the panelle until golden brown, turning in the oil to crisp both sides, about 5 minutes. Drain the fried panelle on brown paper bags and sprinkle with sea salt.

Arrange the fritters on a serving tray and top with pieces of Primo Sale and a pinch of red chilies. Serve immediately, as panelle are at their best piping hot. (I like to encourage guests to make their own sandwiches by serving pieces of good, crusty sesame-seed baguette or rolls alongside the panelle.)

. . . .

WHITE WINE: Sicilian Chardonnay, Vermentino di Gallura, Albariño

Louis XVI, the only King of France ever to be executed, reportedly had a simple last wish before dying: a final taste of Brie de Meaux.

When ripe and ready, the famous cheese from the region of Brie can indeed be the dream of kings. The sweet flavors of roasted fennel, still warm from the oven, work wonders with the earthy mushroom tones of the cheese in this delightful sandwich.

Try to find the best-quality sun-dried tomatoes, generally preserved in high-quality olive oil, which itself becomes a luxury for the pantry.

TO PREPARE THE FENNEL: Preheat the oven to 400°F/200°C/gas 6.

Chop the long stalks off the fennel and save for soups. Wash the bulbs well. Trim away any brown or tough bits. Cut the bulbs in half and then turn, cut-side down, and cut into ¼-in-/6-mm-thick slices. Spread the fennel slices on a baking sheet/tray and drizzle with the olive oil, being sure to coat well. Season with salt and pepper.

Roast the fennel for 25 to 30 minutes, stirring from time to time, until tender and deep golden. Remove from the oven and keep warm.

TO ASSEMBLE THE SANDWICH: Cut a baguette in half horizontally. Cut the cheese into ¼-in-/6-mm-thick slices and place on one side of the bread to cover completely. Heap the roasted fennel atop the cheese, reserving any oil, and then scatter the sun-dried tomatoes over the top. Drizzle the interior of the top piece of the baguette with any reserved cooking oil and then place atop the tomatoes. Cut into eight pieces and serve wrapped in parchment/baking paper.

RED WINE: Lambrusco, Bugey, Beaujolais
WHITE WINE: Riesling, sparkling whites like Prosecco

BRIE DE MEAUX AND ROASTED FENNEL SANDWICH

SERVES 2 TO 4

FOR THE ROASTED FENNEL
2 bulbs fresh fennel

¼ cup/60 ml extra-virgin olive oil

Salt and freshly cracked black pepper

FOR ASSEMBLING THE SANDWICH
1 baguette

12 oz/340 g Brie De Meaux or other good-quality Brie cheese

⅔ cup/115 g best-quality sun-dried tomatoes in oil

Beaufort is a semifirm raw–cow's milk cheese made deep in the French Alps from a mixture of the morning and the evening milk. Richer than Emmental, and milder than Comté, it is one of those rare cheeses other than cream cheese or fromage blanc that pairs perfectly with smoked or cured salmon.

Preheat the oven to 400°F/200°C/gas 6.

Lay the bacon on a baking sheet/tray and bake for 15 to 20 minutes, or until crispy. Discard the fat and place the bacon on paper towels to absorb excess fat.

Toast the slices of bread and then spread some of the crème fraîche on one side of each slice. Build the club sandwich starting with the watercress, cooked bacon, and Beaufort, then another slice of toasted bread, spread with more crème fraîche on the top side, a few slices of avocado, and a slice of gravlax. Squeeze a bit of fresh lemon juice on the fish. Top with the last slice of bread. Skewer the sandwiches with toothpicks and cut into halves or quarters. Serve immediately.

· ·

WHITE WINE: Picpoul, Roero Arneis
RED WINE: Nebbiolo and smoked salmon are a classic pairing that would hold true here

CLUB SANDWICH WITH GRAVLAX, AVOCADO, BACON, AND BEAUFORT

SERVES 2

8 slices bacon

6 slices pain-de-mie or whole-grain bread

¼ cup/60 ml crème fraîche

1 cup/40 g watercress

4 oz/115 g Beaufort cheese, cut into ¼-in/6-mm slices

1 ripe avocado, pitted and peeled

4 oz/115 g gravlax or home-cured salmon

Freshly squeezed lemon juice

MELTED FROMAGER D'AFFINOIS AND MADRANGE HAM SANDWICHES

SERVES 3

1 baguette

8 oz/225 g Fromager d'Affinois cheese

2 oz/55 g Madrange ham, prosciutto cotto, or other high-quality cooked ham/gammon, cut into paper-thin slices

Fromager d'Affinois is hands down the biggest crowd-pleasing cheese there is. It's an ultrarich, 60-percent fat, double-cream cow's milk cheese from the French Rhône-Alps that most people assume is Brie because of its soft white rind and creamy interior. But, without getting too technical, what makes this cheese such a revolutionary invention is a process known as ultrafiltration, which removes water from the pasteurized milk, thereby distributing the fat molecules more evenly throughout the paste. The process also allows the cheese to ripen within two weeks, which means the cheese maintains the sweet buttery flavor of the creamy milk without any of the earthy funk of traditional Brie.

These sandwiches are delicious even without grilling, and their lack of dressings or greens makes them perfect travel food. But warming them in a panini press until the gooey cheese gets even more gooey and takes on the delicate perfume of sweet ham/gammon sends the sandwiches over the moon.

Resist the temptation to add more meat than is called for. This is not a pork sandwich with cheese, but rather a cheese sandwich with the accent of excellent-quality ham/gammon.

Preheat a panini press to medium-high.

Cut the baguette into three equal pieces and slice the pieces in half horizontally. It is best to slice the cheese as you work to avoid a gooey mess. Cut the cheese into slices about ¼ in/6 mm thick and distribute equally among the three bottom pieces of baguette. Drape the ham/gammon over the cheese, distributing it equally as well. I actually allow for some of the meat to drape out of the sides of the sandwich, as those pieces will crisp during grilling.

Replace the tops of the baguettes to close the sandwiches.

Place the sandwiches on the panini press and gently close the lid. After the lid is closed (make sure the tops have not slipped off the sandwiches), press firmly down on the handle for a few seconds. Then release and let the sandwiches cook for 3 to 4 minutes, or until the cheese is melted through and the baguette is crisp and toasted.

Cut the sandwiches in half and serve hot.

· ·

WHITE WINE: lighter, semi-fruity wines such as Riesling, Pinot Grigio, Vermentino di Gallura, Pouilly Fumé; also Prosecco
RED WINE: young Sangiovese, Côte du Rhone, Tempranillo

FRESH RICOTTA TORTA WITH WILD SPRING ONIONS

MAKES ONE 8-IN/20-CM TORTA

My family and I recently visited the Lo Puy goat farm in the Italian Alpine valley of Val Maira, north of Cuneo. We were expecting to simply have a peek at their goats and possibly taste a little cheese. To our surprise, we were greeted with an entire day of food, new friends, and an unforgettable taste of Italian hospitality. They had not been expecting us, so when it came time to eat, we were fortunate enough to be served what was intended to be their simple mountain lunch. A pie made from the morning's homemade goat's milk ricotta and some wild onions that had been picked just outside the kitchen door. The secret to the crust, which was as flaky and delicate as any French pastry, was the homemade *strutto*, or rendered pork fat. Fresh cow's or sheep's milk ricotta will do very nicely in the filling, as will butter for the crust, but if you can get your hands on the original ingredients, the experience is that much better!

cont'd

FOR THE CRUST

1 cup/125 g all-purpose/plain flour

½ tsp salt

⅓ cup/75 g rendered lard or unsalted butter

1 egg

2 tbsp cold water

FOR THE FILLING

1 lb/455 g fresh sheep, goat, or cow's milk ricotta cheese

½ lb/225 g Parmigiano-Reggiano cheese, grated

1 cup/150 g finely chopped wild spring onions or scallions, washed

1 tsp salt

Freshly cracked black pepper

3 eggs, plus 1 egg yolk for brushing

TO PREPARE THE CRUST: Line an 8-in/20.3-cm springform pan with buttered parchment/baking paper. In a mixing bowl, mix together the flour and salt. Blend in the lard with a fork. In a small bowl, mix the egg with the water, add to the flour mixture, and mix until a ball is formed. (This can also be done quickly and easily in a food processor.) Wrap the dough in plastic wrap/cling film and chill for at least 1 hour.

Roll out the dough to a ⅛-in/3-mm thickness and place in the prepared pan, bringing the dough up the sides of the pan. Prick the bottom of the crust and chill for at least 20 minutes. Preheat the oven to 400°F/200°C/gas 6.

TO PREPARE THE FILLING: In a medium bowl, mix together the ricotta, Parmigiano, and onions. Add the salt and pepper, and then add the 3 eggs. Mix well and pour into the prepared crust.

Bake on the middle rack of the oven for 15 minutes and then lower the temperature to 350°F/180°C/gas 4 and bake until golden brown, 30 to 40 minutes more.

Just before the torta is done, brush the top edges of the crust with the egg yolk. Let cool on a wire rack for 10 minutes before releasing from the springform pan. Serve warm or at room temperature.

WHITE WINE: Gavi di Gavi, Pigato
RED WINE: Nebbiolo

This is another recipe, like the Flamiche—Belgian Tart with Bacon, Beer, and Munster (page 152), that has less custard and more cheese! Substitute sautéed wild mushrooms for the zucchini/courgette and omit the ham/gammon for a different version of the tart.

TO PREPARE THE TART SHELL: Put the flour in a bowl with the salt. Add the butter and rub between your fingers to create a coarse meal. Place this mixture in the bowl of a food processor fitted with the blade attachment. Add the crème fraîche and pulse until the dough forms a ball. Stop immediately. (Do not overmix.)

Remove the dough and slam it down on a lightly floured work surface ten or twelve times. (This will help prevent too much rising during the blind baking.) Wrap the dough in plastic wrap/cling film and chill for at least 1 hour.

Roll out the chilled dough on a lightly floured surface to about ⅛ in/3 mm thick. Place the dough in a 10-in/25-cm tart mold, pressing it into the corners and trimming any excess. Prick the bottom all over with a fork and chill for 15 minutes.

Preheat the oven to 350°F/180 C°/gas 4.

Line the inside of the tart shell with parchment/baking paper and fill with pie weights. Blind bake the shell for 15 minutes. Remove the weights and parchment/baking paper and bake for 2 to 3 minutes longer, until the crust is no longer wet. (If the dough puffs up a bit, flatten it down with a metal spatula.)

cont'd

ZUCCHINI AND CAMEMBERT TART

MAKES ONE 10-IN/25-CM TART

FOR THE TART SHELL
2 cups/255 g all-purpose/plain flour

Pinch of salt

½ cup/115 g butter, cut into cubes

⅔ cup/165 ml crème fraîche

TO PREPARE THE FILLING: Wash the zucchini/courgettes, cut in half lengthwise, and then cut again into half-circle slices ¼ in/6 mm thick.

Heat the olive oil in a large frying pan over high heat and sauté the zucchini/courgettes in a couple batches, not stirring too often so that deep golden brown spots are allowed to form, 2 to 3 minutes.

In a bowl, mix together the eggs, cream, salt, and a few grindings of pepper.

Scatter the ham over the bottom of the blind-baked tart shell. Add the zucchini/courgettes and spread out evenly. Pour the egg mixture over the vegetables and ham. Cut the Camembert into eight pieces and distribute evenly over the tart.

Bake for about 40 minutes, or until golden brown and set. Let cool for 15 minutes before carefully removing from the pan. Serve warm or at room temperature.

WHITE WINE: Austrian Riesling, Chardonnay

FOR THE FILLING

3 medium zucchini/courgettes

¼ cup/60 ml extra-virgin olive oil

3 eggs

¾ cup/180 ml heavy/double cream

Pinch of salt

Freshly cracked black pepper

2 oz/55 g Madrange ham, cut into thin slices and roughly chopped

One 8-oz/225-g wheel ripe Camembert cheese

FLAMICHE—BELGIAN TART WITH BACON, BEER, AND MUNSTER

MAKES ONE 10-IN/25-CM TART

FOR THE TART SHELL

2 cups/255 g all-purpose/plain flour

Pinch of salt

½ cup/115 g butter, cut into cubes

⅔ cup/165 ml crème fraîche

Legend says that flamiche was created by a farmer's wife from the Belgian city of Romedenne who slipped on her way to sell her farm goods at the market. The products in her basket, including butter, eggs, and cheese, mixed together. She ran to a friend who was baking bread at that moment. There she made a base from some of the dough, added the mixture from her basket, and put her creation in the oven. In Italy, such a pie is often called *pasticcio*, meaning a "big mess," which brings to mind much the same imagery. This version of flamiche is made without eggs, but is still decadently rich thanks to a generous amount of crème fraîche.

Although Munster is from Alsace and not Belgium, its stinky goodness is fantastic with the flavors of bacon, onion, and beer. A milder yet equally delicious variation of this tart can be made with Reblochon cheese in place of the Munster.

TO PREPARE THE TART SHELL: Put the flour in a bowl with the salt. Add the butter and rub between your fingers to create a coarse meal. Place this mixture in the bowl of a food processor fitted with the blade attachment. Add the crème fraîche and pulse until the dough forms a ball. Stop immediately. (Do not overmix.)

Remove the dough and slam it down on a lightly floured work surface ten or twelve times. (This will help prevent too much rising during the blind baking.) Wrap in plastic wrap/cling film and chill for at least 1 hour.

Roll out the chilled dough on a lightly floured surface to about ⅛ in/3 mm thick. Place the dough in a 10-in/25-cm tart mold, pressing it into the corners and trimming any excess. Prick the bottom all over with a fork and chill for 15 minutes.

Preheat the oven to 350°F/180 C°/gas 4.

Line the inside of the tart shell with parchment/baking paper and fill with pie weights. Blind bake the shell for 15 minutes. Remove the weights and parchment/baking paper and continue baking for 2 to 3 minutes longer, until the crust is no longer wet. (If the dough puffs up a bit, flatten it down with a metal spatula.)

TO PREPARE THE FILLING: In a large sauté pan, cook the bacon over medium heat until crisp. Discard the fat and set aside the bacon.

Add the butter and onions to the pan. Sweat the onions over low heat for about 15 minutes, or until translucent and just starting to turn golden. Add the garlic, cook for a minute or so, and then add the beer, half of the Munster, and the crème fraîche. Simmer for 3 minutes. Season with plenty of salt and pepper.

Scatter the bacon evenly in the prepared tart shell. Pour the beer-Munster mixture over the bacon, and top with the remaining Munster. Bake for 35 to 40 minutes, or until golden brown. Let cool for 10 minutes before carefully removing from the pan. Serve warm or at room temperature.

· ·

WHITE WINE: Chardonnay and the whites of Jura

FOR THE FILLING

8 oz/225 g smoked bacon, chopped

2 tbsp butter

3 small yellow onions, sliced

2 garlic cloves, crushed and peeled

3 tbsp Belgian beer, such as Chimay

8 oz/225 g Munster cheese,
broken into walnut-size pieces

¾ cup/180 ml crème fraîche

Salt and freshly cracked black pepper

SAVORY CHOCOLATE FETTUCCINE WITH MASCARPONE AND LEMON / 157

CANNELLONI WITH BURRATA AND PROSCIUTTO / 160

LASAGNA WITH ASPARAGUS AND BURRATA / 162

RIGATONCINI WITH SAUSAGE, FRESH RICOTTA, AND ORANGE ZEST / 165

FARFALLE WITH FRESH GOAT CHEESE,
BROCCOLINI, AND CRUNCHY SHALLOTS / 166

HANDMADE GARGANELLI WITH GORGONZOLA AND WALNUTS / 168

GNOCCHETTI WITH GOLDEN PECORINO AND SAFFRON SAUCE / 170

SUNSHINE RAVIOLI / 172

RISOTTO CON UBRIACO / 174

RISOTTO CAKES WITH FRESH ROBIOLA / 176

GREEN APPLE SPAETZLE WITH SBRINZ / 178

PASTA AND RISOTTO

One glance at this section may have you wondering how a book about cooking with cheese would not have a recipe for macaroni and cheese. Whether an old-school béchamel-based tube pasta with cheddar, a baked ziti in meaty tomato sauce with strings of melted mozzarella, or something more mysterious, inspired by the truffle-craze of the day, I love a baked pasta and cheese as much as anyone. But mac 'n' cheese is one of those dishes I am quite sure has been well represented in our blog-filled, television-bombarded, cookbook-hoarding universe, and needs no insights from me. (Although I do recommend using an extra aged Gouda like Beemster the next time you make it!)

"Pasta should not be an excuse to eat sauce," said Carlo Middione. And the same is true of cheese. The pasta, especially pasta made by hand, should be the focus. Sauce and cheese are there to add texture, flavor, and contours to the perfectly cooked noodle. Having said that, you should feel free to add or subtract the amounts I put forth, as you know better what works for you!

WINE NOTE

Wines are paired to the sauce with pastas. The following is a list of wines that go well with the traditional sauce bases.

- **OLIVE OIL SAUCE**—Sancerre, Sauvignon Blanc, and Greco di Tufo are whites whose acidity cuts through the oils.

- **TOMATO SAUCE**—Barbera, Dolcetto d'Alba, Valpolicella, or reds with low tannins and tangy acidity soften the tomato acids, leaving the pretty little fruits to showcase.

- **CREAM SAUCE**—White wines like Vermentino, un-oaked Chardonnay, and off-dry Rieslings work best as the cream of the sauce softens the acidity of the wine, while the acidity of the wine neutralizes the fats.

- **MEAT SAUCE**—Robust red wines such as Nebbiolo-based wines and Sangiovese blends have tannins that attack the fats in the meat, and these same fats soften the tannins, revealing the beauty of the fruits.

When the cocoa bean was first brought to Europe in the 1500s, it wasn't immediately seized upon as a dessert spice. Cocoa was used to flavor game and meat sauces and still is today in dishes from Rome like Cinghiale in Agrodolce, a wild boar stew made with bittersweet chocolate, pine nuts, prunes, and orange zest.

The following is a recipe for fresh pasta made with flour, eggs, and cocoa, and it is very much a savory dish. The amount of cocoa is small—just enough to create a beautiful dough that looks and feels like suede and has a perfume of cocoa more at the end than right up front. It is the same dough I use on Valentine's Day to make heart-shaped ravioli filled with roasted squash for my wife.

Mascarpone is a triple-cream cow's milk cheese that originated in the early seventeenth century and is usually thought of as a dessert cheese. Its relationship with chocolate is famous, and its slight tang works beautifully with these ribbons of cocoa pasta. The scent of lemon lightens this decadent dish, but I still would serve the pasta as a smaller course of a larger meal, as it is quite rich.

cont'd

SAVORY CHOCOLATE FETTUCCINE WITH MASCARPONE AND LEMON

SERVES 6

TO PREPARE THE PASTA: In a large bowl, whisk together the flour and cocoa. Make a well in the center. Break the eggs into the center and beat with a fork, gradually incorporating a bit of the flour from the sides of the well until a sticky dough is formed. Turn the dough out onto a lightly floured work surface and knead, adding a bit of flour if needed until the dough is smooth and elastic, 3 to 5 minutes. Cover the dough in plastic wrap/cling film and let sit at room temperature for at least 30 minutes.

Working with half of the dough at a time, use a pasta maker to roll out long sheets 1/16 in/2 mm thick onto a lightly floured surface. Cut into sheets about 10 in/25 cm long. Cut the sheets into fettuccine with the appropriate attachment. Continue with the remaining dough.

TO PREPARE THE SAUCE: In a large pot, bring plenty of salted water to a boil. Gently heat the butter in a large frying pan until just sizzling but not turning brown. Remove from the heat and add the mascarpone all at once. Do not stir. Pour the butter and mascarpone into a large, preheated serving bowl. Zest the lemon into the bowl along with a few grindings of pepper.

TO ASSEMBLE THE DISH: Cook the pasta in the boiling water until al dente, anywhere from 45 to 60 seconds. You may have to do this quickly in two batches, depending on the size of your pot of boiling water. Drain and add the pasta to the serving bowl along with half of the Parmigiano. Stir quickly to combine and melt the mascarpone into a velvety sauce. Serve immediately in the bowl at the table topped with the remaining Parmigiano.

. . . .

WHITE WINE: Soave
RED WINE: Valpolicella, Bardolino

FOR THE PASTA
3½ cups/440 g all-purpose/plain flour, plus more if needed

3 tbsp Dutch-process cocoa

4 eggs

FOR THE SAUCE
4 tbsp/55 g unsalted butter

1 lb/455 g mascarpone cheese

2 lemons, for zesting

Freshly cracked black pepper

FOR ASSEMBLING THE DISH
¾ cup/75 g grated Parmigiano-Reggiano

CANNELLONI WITH BURRATA AND PROSCIUTTO

SERVES 8

FOR THE PASTA
3½ cups/440 g all-purpose/plain flour,
plus more if needed

4 eggs

FOR THE SAUCE
4 tbsp/60 ml extra-virgin olive oil

1 small yellow onion, minced

2 garlic cloves, peeled

1 lb/455 g fresh ripe tomatoes, chopped, or
high-quality canned, crushed

2 fresh basil leaves

Salt and freshly cracked black pepper

Here again we find Burrata as more than just a creamy mozzarella for a tomato salad. The melting qualities of Burrata are phenomenal, whether atop a simple pizza or stuffed into pillows of fresh pasta. This is a huge crowd-pleaser, either as a main dish or as a richly satisfying pasta course. For large groups, the recipe can be doubled and is worth making in advance; otherwise, I prefer to make and bake it all in the same go.

TO PREPARE THE PASTA: Place the flour in a large bowl and make a well in the center. Break the eggs into the center and beat with a fork, gradually incorporating a bit of the flour from the sides of the well until a sticky dough is formed. Turn the dough out onto a lightly floured work surface and knead, adding a bit of flour if needed until the dough is smooth and elastic, 3 to 5 minutes. Cover the dough in plastic wrap/cling film and let sit at room temperature for at least 30 minutes.

TO PREPARE THE SAUCE: Meanwhile heat the olive oil in a large frying pan over medium heat. Add the onion and the garlic and cook for 10 to 12 minutes, or until the onion is translucent and the garlic is golden on both sides. Add the tomatoes and basil and season well with salt and pepper. Turn up the heat and bring the sauce to a rapid boil, then lower the heat to medium and simmer for 10 minutes, stirring occasionally. Add a splash of pasta water if the sauce is too tight.

Remove from the heat and let cool slightly. Pass through a food mill or puree in a food processor fitted with a blade attachment. (Take care when blending hot food.) Transfer the sauce to a clean bowl.

TO PREPARE THE FILLING: Place the Burrata and ricotta in a large bowl and, using your fingers, tear up the Burrata and mix with the ricotta. Add the prosciutto, Parmigiano, and parsley. Season with salt and pepper and mix thoroughly until well combined.

TO ASSEMBLE THE DISH: When the dough is rested, roll out the pasta with a pasta machine into large sheets roughly ¹⁄₁₆ in/2 mm thick. Cut the sheets into rectangles 4 by 5 in/ 10 by 12 cm, for a total of 16 rectangles.

In a large pot, bring plenty of salted water to a boil.

Boil a few pasta rectangles at a time for 1 minute or so, until al dente. Immediately plunge the rectangles into a bowl of ice water to stop them from cooking further, and then remove, pat dry with a kitchen towel, and lay out on a counter.

Divide the filling among the rectangles of cooked pasta, placing the filling directly in the center of each one. Fold over the two shorter sides of the pasta to form a tube. (Cannelloni can be prepared to this point up to a day in advance but should be removed from the refrigerator 30 minutes before proceeding.)

Preheat the oven to 400°F/200°C/gas 6.

Lightly grease two 8-by-11-in/20-by-28-cm low-sided baking dishes with the olive oil (or eight individual ceramic gratin dishes).

Pour 1 cup of sauce into the bottom of each dish (or ¼ cup/60 ml into the individual dishes). Lay the cannelloni seam-side down in the dishes, slightly overlapping them as needed. (For the individual dishes, lay two cannelloni in each dish.)

Cover with an equal amount of sauce per dish. Do not worry about covering the pasta completely, as the unsauced edges will crisp beautifully. (Reserve any leftover sauce in the refrigerator for another use within the next few days.)

Whisk the cream in a medium bowl until just beginning to thicken. Drizzle the thickened cream over the tomato sauce. Sprinkle the Parmigiano over the top and season again with salt.

Bake the cannelloni for 25 to 30 minutes, or until bubbling and hot throughout. Crisp burned spots here and there are very much desirable.

Serve immediately.

FOR THE FILLING

12 oz/340 g fresh Burrata cheese

6 oz/225 g fresh ricotta cheese

2 oz/55 g prosciutto di Parma, chopped

⅓ cup/30 g grated Parmigiano-Reggiano cheese

¼ cup/15 g fresh flat-leaf parsley, chopped

Salt and freshly cracked black pepper

FOR ASSEMBLING THE DISH

Extra-virgin olive oil, for greasing

¾ cup/180 ml heavy/double cream

¾ cup/75 g grated Parmigiano-Reggiano cheese

Salt

WHITE WINE: Lacryma Christi, Greco di Tufo
RED WINE: Aglianico

LASAGNA WITH ASPARAGUS AND BURRATA

SERVES 4 TO 6

FOR THE PASTA
2 cups/255 g all-purpose/plain flour

2 eggs

2 egg yolks

FOR THE FILLING
14 oz/400 g medium asparagus

8 oz/230 g fresh Burrata cheese

¼ cup/25 g grated Parmigiano-Reggiano cheese

Salt and freshly cracked black pepper

Either flown in fresh from Puglia, or made locally by a domestic artisan near you, Burrata is becoming more widely available all over the world. Here's a chance to see one of the many ways Burrata can be utilized in the kitchen, where it single-handedly takes on the role that a béchamel would normally play. It is a cheese that should be purchased and consumed as close as possible to the time it was made.

TO PREPARE THE PASTA: Put the flour in a medium bowl and create a well in the center. Add the eggs and egg yolks and beat them with a fork, incorporating a little flour from the sides of the mound at a time, until a sticky mass is formed. Turn the dough out onto a lightly floured work surface and knead the dough until smooth and pliable.

Wrap the dough in plastic wrap/cling film and let rest at room temperature for 1 hour.

TO PREPARE THE FILLING: Meanwhile, trim the tips of the asparagus and set aside. Blanch the spears of asparagus in plenty of salted boiling water for 8 to 10 minutes, or until very tender. Remove from the water, shock in a bowl of ice water, and drain. Add the reserved asparagus tips to the boiling water and cook for 4 to 5 minutes, or until cooked but still firm. Shock the tips and drain.

In the bowl of a food processor fitted with the blade attachment, puree the cooked asparagus spears (not the tips) until smooth. Add the Burrata and the Parmigiano. Puree until smooth. Season with salt and pepper.

When the dough is rested, roll out with a pasta machine to a thickness of $\frac{1}{32}$ in/1 mm. Cut into sheets roughly 6 by 12 in/15 by 30 cm.

Boil the pasta sheets in the same water the asparagus was cooked in for about 1 minute, or until al dente. Shock the pasta in ice water quickly and then remove and pat dry with a clean kitchen towel.

cont'd

FOR ASSEMBLING THE LASAGNA

¾ cup/75 g Parmigiano-Reggiano cheese

¼ cup/60 ml cup extra-virgin olive oil

4 oz/115 g prosciutto di Parma, cut into thin slices (optional)

4 oz/115 g fresh Burrata cheese

TO ASSEMBLE THE LASAGNA: Preheat the oven to 425°F/ 220°C/gas 7.

Spoon ¼ cup/60 ml of the asparagus-Burrata filling into the bottom of a lightly buttered baking dish. Place a sheet of cooked pasta over the filling and then cover with another ¼ cup/60 ml of the filling. Scatter a few of the cooked asparagus tips over the filling and then sprinkle a bit of the Parmigiano and a drizzle of the olive oil. Place another cooked sheet of pasta on top and continue layering, ending with the last of the sauce. Tear the Burrata into golf ball–size pieces and scatter over the top. Sprinkle with the remaining Parmigiano and the last of the olive oil.

Place on the top rack of the oven and cook for 20 to 25 minutes, or until hot and bubbling with golden melted pools of Burrata and crisp edges of pasta.

Remove from the oven and let stand for 10 minutes before serving. Cut into squares and place individual pieces on warm dinner plates. If using the prosciutto, gently drape a few slices around the edges of the lasagna and serve.

WHITE WINE: un-oaked Chardonnay, Verdicchio, Prosecco
RED WINE: Aglianico, Sangiovese

Inspired by my mentor, Carlo Middione, whose knowledge of pasta knows no equal, this dish not only shows off the creaminess of ultra-fresh, high-quality ricotta but also gives you a chance to find the very best Italian sausages you can lay your hands on. I add the orange zest at the end to brighten the whole dish.

Preheat the oven to 375°F/190°C/gas 5.

Place the sausages on a baking sheet/tray and roast for 25 to 30 minutes, or until the internal temperature on a thermometer reads 150°F/65°C. Remove from the oven and let cool. Cut the sausages on an angle into six pieces each.

Bring plenty of salted water to a boil. Add the pasta to the water and cook, stirring often, for 9 to 12 minutes, or until al dente.

Meanwhile, heat the olive oil in a large sauté pan to hot but not smoking. Add the sausages along with the garlic. Sauté over medium-high heat for 4 to 5 minutes, or until the sausage is crisp and the garlic is golden.

Splash in a tablespoon or so of the pasta water to stop the garlic from cooking further. Remove from the heat and add the ricotta to the sausages. Drain the cooked pasta and add to the pan (or turn everything out into a large, warm serving bowl if the pan is not big enough). Add half of the pecorino and toss well. Zest the oranges directly onto the pasta and toss again. Season with salt and pepper.

Add a drizzle more of extra-virgin olive oil if needed. Serve hot with the remaining pecorino at the table.

WHITE WINE: wines with fruit and acid like Riesling and Soave
RED WINE: Lacrima di'Morro, Salice Salentino

RIGATONCINI WITH SAUSAGE, FRESH RICOTTA, AND ORANGE ZEST

SERVES 4

1 lb/455 g whole Italian sweet sausages

1 lb/455 g dried rigatoncini pasta

6 tbsp/90 ml extra-virgin olive oil, plus more if needed

4 garlic cloves, peeled

1 lb/455 g fresh ricotta cheese

1 cup/100 g grated Pecorino Romano cheese

2 oranges, for zesting

Salt and freshly cracked black pepper

FARFALLE WITH FRESH GOAT CHEESE, BROCCOLINI, AND CRUNCHY SHALLOTS

SERVES 2

½ cup/120 ml extra-virgin olive oil

1 large shallot, peeled and cut into thin slices

8 oz/225 g farfalle pasta

4 oz/115 g broccolini, trimmed of any woody ends

¼ cup/30 g pine nuts, toasted

Salt and freshly cracked black pepper

4 oz/115 g fresh goat cheese

½ cup/50 g grated Pecorino Romano cheese, plus more for serving

Time spent on a rapid-fire hot line of a busy restaurant has taught me an appreciation for the ability to multitask. This is the kind of simple yet delicious dish born out of a need for dinner in a hurry met with a quick raid of the icebox and pantry.

In a large pot, bring plenty of salted water to a boil.

Heat the olive oil in a medium frying pan over high heat. Add the shallot and cook, stirring often, for 2 to 3 minutes, or until deep golden brown and crispy (be careful not to burn). Remove from the pan and set aside in a small bowl, reserving the oil.

Add the pasta to the boiling water and stir. Add the broccolini at the same time and boil for about 4 minutes, or until cooked but still quite firm. With a pair of tongs, remove the broccolini from the water to a cutting board and continue cooking the pasta until al dente.

While the pasta is cooking, roughly chop the cooked broccolini. Add the oil used to cook the shallots back into the sauté pan and turn the heat to high. Add the broccolini and pine nuts and cook for 2 to 3 minutes, or until the broccolini is slightly gilded. Season well with salt and pepper.

When the pasta is al dente, drain and place in a large serving bowl. Scatter the goat cheese over the cooked broccolini and pine nuts and then pour the mixture over the cooked pasta. Add the grated pecorino cheese and mix well. Divide the pasta among individual serving bowls, scatter fried shallots over the top, and serve, passing pecorino at the table.

. . . .

WHITE WINE: Vermentino di Gallura, Friulano
RED WINE: Montepulciano d'Abruzzo, Montalcino, Montefalco Rosso

HANDMADE GARGANELLI WITH GORGONZOLA AND WALNUTS

SERVES 6

FOR THE PASTA

2 cups/255 g all-purpose/plain flour

½ cup/50 g finely grated Parmigiano-Reggiano cheese

3 eggs

FOR THE SAUCE

4 tbsp/55 g unsalted butter

¾ cup/85 g walnut halves, roughly chopped

2 cups/480 ml heavy/double cream

6 oz/170 g Gorgonzola dolce latte cheese

FOR THE ASSEMBLING DISH
1 cup/100 g Parmigiano-Reggiano, grated

Salt and freshly cracked black pepper

Garganelli pasta is basically a form of penne pasta from Emilia Romagna that's made with eggs instead of water, and sometimes cheese is added to the pasta dough as well. The noodles are traditionally made by rolling squares of pasta around a stick to form a tube. These tubes are then rolled across a special comb, although gnocchi boards, which have become more readily available in specialty kitchen shops, work just as well.

There is also very-good-quality garganelli from Rustichella d'Abruzzo, which is available in fine food stores or online, but nothing beats fresh pasta for a cream-based sauce.

This is an uber-rich dish, making it a nice starter before serving roasted game birds or meats.

TO PREPARE THE PASTA: Place the flour and Parmigiano in a large bowl and whisk together to combine. Form a well in the center and break the eggs into it.

Beat the eggs with a fork and gradually start incorporating the flour-cheese mixture into the eggs until a sticky dough forms. Turn the dough out onto a lightly floured work surface and knead for 3 to 5 minutes, or until the dough is shiny and soft. Cover the dough with plastic wrap/cling film and let rest at room temperature for at least an hour.

Roll out the dough into ⅟₁₆-in/2-mm sheets with a pasta machine. Cut the dough into 1½-in/4-cm squares. Place the squares on a ridged gnocchi board. Then, starting from one corner, wrap each square around a clean pencil and roll across the board to close and form ridges. Gently slide the garganelli off the pencil and onto a lightly floured kitchen towel. Continue until all the dough is shaped.

In a large pot, bring plenty of salted water to a boil.

TO PREPARE THE SAUCE: Melt the butter in a large sauté pan over medium heat. Add the walnuts and cook for 3 to 4 minutes, or until toasty and aromatic but not burned. Add the cream all at once, stir, and raise the heat to medium-high. Watch carefully as the cream begins to boil and rise. Turn down the heat before the cream spills over the edge of the pan, reducing to a simmer. Continue cooking until the sauce is reduced by a third, 5 to 6 minutes. Remove from the heat and crumble the gorgonzola over the sauce.

TO ASSEMBLE THE DISH: Add the pasta to the boiling water and cook, stirring often, for about 5 minutes, or until the pasta is cooked but very al dente. Drain the cooked pasta and add to the sauce. Add half of the grated Parmigiano and stir to coat the pasta well with the sauce. Season with salt and pepper. Transfer to individual plates or one large dish, top with the remaining Parmigiano, and serve immediately.

WHITE WINE: Vermentino di Gallura, off-dry Riesling, Friulano
RED WINE: non-tannic Valpolicella

GNOCCHETTI WITH GOLDEN PECORINO AND SAFFRON SAUCE

SERVES 4

1 lb/455 g gnocchetti or malloreddus pasta

11 oz/310 g fresh pecorino cheese, cut into small cubes

8 to 12 saffron threads

Salt and freshly cracked black pepper

This simple recipe relies on the purity and high quality of the ingredients. Look for a young pecorino that is soft to the touch, almost Monterey Jack–like in texture. Sardinian pecorino is an obvious choice, although there are amazing varieties from all over Italy, not the least of which is young Primo Sale. Sardinia is responsible for 60 percent of Italy's saffron production, and the precious spice has been cultivated on the island since the thirteenth century. Originally used for medicinal purposes, its value in the Renaissance went from the apothecary to the kitchen, although the Arab use of saffron and its influence on the cuisine of Sardinia date back to the fall of the Roman Empire.

In a large pot, bring plenty of salted water to a boil. Add the pasta and cook until al dente, stirring often. Place a heat-proof bowl over the boiling water and add the cheese and saffron. Stir the cheese and saffron with a wooden spoon for 7 or 8 minutes, or until melted and golden. Drain the pasta, add to the melted cheese, and mix until the pasta is evenly coated with cheese. Season with salt and plenty of pepper and serve immediately.

WHITE WINE: Vermentino di Gallura
RED WINE: Cannonau

SUNSHINE RAVIOLI

SERVES 6 TO 8
(MAKES ABOUT 100 RAVIOLI)

FOR THE DOUGH
4 cups/500 g durum wheat flour,
plus more if needed

5 eggs

2 tbsp extra-virgin olive oil

FOR THE FILLING
2 large oranges, for zesting

1½ lb/680 g fresh ricotta cheese

½ lb/225 g fresh Pantaleo cheese

Salt and freshly cracked black pepper

2 eggs

FOR ASSEMBLING THE DISH
8 tbsp/115 g butter, at room temperature

2 cups/200 g grated Pantaleo cheese

The wall around the city of Perugia in Italy's glorious Umbria region was built in the year A.D. 1. At Enoteca Aladino, an underground wine cellar-turned-restaurant, guests sit among bottles and bottles of wine tucked into cutouts of these very walls. The chef, at least when I ate there, was Sardinian and would find little ways of expressing it from time to time with recipes like this one for delicate little pillows of handmade pasta filled with fresh ricotta and toasted orange zest.

I have added Pantaleo cheese to the recipe, using it in the filling and for grating over the top of the dish. Aged for more than 100 days, Pantaleo is a delicious, nutty raw–goat's milk cheese from Sardinia that works as well in the kitchen as it does on a cheese board. Fiore Sardo can be used if Pantaleo is unavailable.

TO PREPARE THE DOUGH: Place the flour in a medium bowl and make a well in the center. Break the eggs into the well and add the olive oil. Using a fork, beat the eggs and oil together, gradually gathering some of the flour from the sides of the well until a sticky dough is formed. Turn the dough out onto a lightly floured work surface and knead for about 5 minutes, until the dough is elastic and shiny. Add a bit more flour if it's too sticky. Wrap the dough in plastic wrap/cling film and let rest at room temperature for 1 hour.

TO PREPARE THE FILLING: Preheat the oven to 400°F/ 200°C/gas 6.

Line a baking sheet/tray with parchment/baking paper and zest the oranges onto the paper. Toast in the oven for 8 to 10 minutes, or until dried and crunchy. Remove from the oven and shake the zest off the paper into a medium bowl. Be sure to get all of the zest. Add the ricotta and Pantaleo. Stir well to combine, seasoning with salt and pepper. Add the eggs and mix well.

TO ASSEMBLE THE DISH: Using a pasta machine, roll the dough into two long, thin sheets, about ⅟₃₂ in/1 mm. Spread the filling evenly over one sheet of pasta with an inverted metal spatula, leaving a ⅛-in/3-mm border around the edges. Place the second sheet of pasta over the filling and press down gently. Brush the edges with a small amount of water and press to seal. Roll a ravioli pin over the two sheets to form little pillows and then cut with a fluted pasta cutter. (Or working more free-form, use a fluted pasta cutter to cut out squares in rows; about 25 rows of 4 will make roughly 100 ravioli.) Place the cut ravioli onto baking sheets/trays lined with lightly floured kitchen towels or parchment/baking paper.

In a large pot, bring plenty of salted water to a boil. Cook the ravioli a few at a time (the water should always remain boiling) for 3 to 4 minutes, or until al dente. Drain and toss with the butter and the grated Pantaleo. Serve immediately.

WHITE WINE: Vermentino di Gallura
RED WINE: Cannonau

RISOTTO CON UBRIACO

SERVES 2

3 cups/720 ml best-quality chicken stock

Salt and freshly cracked black pepper

2 tbsp unsalted butter, plus 3 tbsp at room temperature for finishing risotto

2 shallots, finely chopped

1 cup/150 g Carnaroli or Arborio rice

1 cup/240 ml dry white wine

¾ cup/75 g grated Parmigiano-Reggiano cheese

2 oz/55 g Ubriaco cheese, cut into thin slices

Ubriaco means "drunken" in Italian, and in this case refers to a cheese from Italy's Veneto region. The cheese, which is traditionally made from cow's milk, is soaked in wine and covered with crushed grape skins. It is an old tradition, and several different versions of Ubriaco can be found, all using different varieties of wine—from Amarone to Prosecco—and different types of milk depending on the region.

Briscole al Barbera is an Ubriaco cheese made in Verona, washed in Barbera wine, and named for the card game Briscole, as this is a wonderful cheese to snack on during such a game. Ubriaco cheeses are ideal for cooking, and the scent of the wine is more pronounced when the cheese is heated. This is a recipe for a classic risotto with sheets of melted Ubriaco layed on top. It is a delicious meal on its own or served alongside roasted guinea or game hen.

On the off chance that any risotto is left over, Risotto Cakes with Fresh Robiola (page 176) is a fantastic way to use it up, perhaps the next day for a light lunch with a bitter green salad.

Bring the stock to a simmer in a stockpot over medium-low heat. Season with salt and pepper. Meanwhile, in a deep heavy-bottomed frying pan, heat the 2 tbsp butter over medium heat. Add the shallots and cook until soft and translucent, about 10 minutes.

Add the rice and cook over medium-high heat for about 1 minute, stirring constantly to coat with the butter. Add the wine and stir for 30 seconds, or until the wine is absorbed.

Using a ½-cup/120-ml ladle, add one ladle of simmering stock to the mixture in the pan. Stir until most but not all of the liquid is absorbed. Add another ladle, stirring constantly, repeating the process until the risotto is tender and creamy or, as the Venetians say, *al onda*, meaning "like the waves." This may take up to 40 minutes or so, but there are few greater rewards for patience than perfectly cooked risotto.

Remove from the heat and add the Parmigiano and the remaining butter. Shake the pan vigorously to move the risotto around and distribute the butter and cheese throughout the risotto to create a creamy and elegantly finished product. Season with salt and divide into individual heated bowls.

Drape slices of the Ubriaco over the plated risotto and serve immediately.

RED WINE: Barbera d'Alba, Barolo, Sagrantino Montefalco

RISOTTO CAKES WITH FRESH ROBIOLA

MAKES 10 RISOTTO CAKES

2½ cups/255 g risotto (see page 174)

1 egg

3 cubes fresh Robiola, 3½ oz/100 g each

3 tbsp unsalted butter, plus more as needed

2 tbsp extra-virgin olive oil, plus more as needed

The fresh Robiola I like for this recipe is a double-cream cow's milk cheese made by Fattorie Osella in Piemonte, Italy. A goat-milk version is available for a small window of time in the year, but I love the sweet, buttery taste of the cow's milk Robiola.

Sold in 3½-oz/100-g cubes, with an airy texture of whipped cream cheese and a delightful tang, Osella Robiola is widely available, although many other Robiola cheeses would work well, including the sheep-, cow-, and goat-milk version known as Robiola tre latte.

Mix the cold risotto with the egg until well blended. Shape ¼ cup/60 ml of the risotto into a patty. Cut each Robiola cube into four pieces. (You will end up with a couple of extra pieces; they should not be shared with anyone but, instead, greedily devoured with slices of fresh peach or a chunk of crusty bread.) Place a piece of the Robiola in the middle of the rice patty and close the rice around it to seal, reshaping as necessary to create a disc 3 in/7.5 cm in diameter and ½ in/12 mm thick. Repeat with the remaining risotto and cheese to make a total of ten cakes.

Preheat the oven to 200°F/95°C.

In a large frying pan over medium-high heat, heat the butter and olive oil until sizzling. Working in batches to avoid crowding the pan, fry the risotto cakes until golden brown and crisp on the first sides, about 2 minutes. Being very careful, gently turn the cakes over with a slotted spatula and fry them on the second side until golden brown, about 2 minutes longer. The Robiola may begin to ooze out a bit, which is a good indication that the cakes are ready. Transfer the cakes to a baking sheet/tray as they are finished and keep warm in the oven. Cook the remaining cakes in the same way, adding a bit more clean oil and butter to the pan as needed. Serve hot.

WHITE WINE: Roero Arneis
RED WINE: Barbera d'Alba, Dolcetto

GREEN APPLE SPAETZLE WITH SBRINZ

SERVES 3 OR 4

2½ cups/315 g all-purpose/plain flour,
plus more as needed

½ tsp salt

3 eggs

½ cup/120 ml apple juice, plus more as needed

1 tart green apple, such as Granny Smith

4 tbsp/55 g best-quality butter

6 oz/170 g Sbrinz cheese

Sbrinz is a delightfully fruity hard cheese from central Switzerland that has been traditionally made for centuries. Parmigiano-Reggiano may be known as the king of cheeses in Italy, but Sbrinz is considered the father of hard cheeses by the Swiss. And just as with Parmigiano-Reggiano, Sbrinz is made with whole raw milk rather than skimmed milk, producing deep, nutty flavors.

Spaetzle is fast becoming one of my favorite things to make and eat. Delicate, golden dumplings are tossed with the best-quality butter and, in this case, a generous showering of cheese. The addition of tart green apple makes this the ultimate accompaniment to breaded pork chops or roasted pork loin!

In a large bowl, whisk together the flour and salt. Make a well in the center. Break the eggs into the well and add the apple juice. Beat the eggs with a fork, mixing them with the juice, and begin to gather some of the flour from the sides of the well. Continue incorporating the flour into the wet ingredients until a sticky batter forms. You may need to add a touch more flour or juice before you have a smooth dough wet enough to pass through a spaetzle maker.

Peel and core the apple, then finely grate it into the spaetzle batter and stir to combine.

Bring plenty of salted water to a boil in a large pot. When the water is boiling, pass 1 cup/240 ml of the batter through the spaetzle maker, letting the spaetzle fall into the water. Use a rubber spatula to force it through the holes and continue until all the batter has gone through. Boil the spaetzle for 1 to 2 minutes, or until firm. Remove the dumplings from the boiling water with a strainer or slotted spoon and plunge into a bowl of ice water to stop them from over-cooking. Immediately remove them from the ice water and place in a separate bowl. Continue with the rest of the batter. (Spaetzle can be made up to this point several hours ahead and dressed with melted butter or a drizzle of extra-virgin olive oil to prevent them from sticking.)

When ready to serve, melt the butter in a large sauté pan over high heat. Add the boiled spaetzle and sauté, shaking the pan from time to time but allowing little golden spots to appear here and there, 2 to 3 minutes. Scatter the Sbrinz over the spaetzle and stir to combine well. Place the spaetzle into a warm ceramic dish and serve immediately.

. . . .

WHITE WINE: Riesling, especially if served with breaded pork chops
RED WINE: St. Laurent, Gamay, Beaujolais

TOMATO-BRAISED MEATBALLS WITH MELTING MOZZARELLA / 183

SAUSAGES STUFFED WITH TRUFFLE CHEESE / 186

SHEPHERD'S PIE WITH ROQUEFORT MASH / 188

BREADED LAMB CHOPS WITH RONCAL AND FRESH MINT / 191

PORK LOIN SKEWERS WITH AGED GOUDA AND APRICOT MUSTARD / 193

GRILLED RIB-EYE STEAKS WITH ROGUE RIVER BLUE / 195

ROASTED QUAIL WITH BREAD AND ROCCOLO CHEESE SAUCE / 196

POUSSIN WITH GRUYÈRE DE COMTÉ / 198

MEATS AND FOWL

I must say that I feel as strongly about sourcing the very-best-quality meat, poultry, and fish for my family as I do about sourcing good-quality cheeses. The argument that meat from better-fed, humanely raised, and non-hormone-injected livestock is cost prohibitive to most is not a good enough reason to settle for the factory-produced, stress-filled, anonymous product available for less money. It's all about priorities: I prefer to eat a little less of a better thing, if for no other reason than flavor.

The same is true for cheese. Little amounts of the best-quality cheese are not only more enjoyable, but I propose that the flavors of well-made artisanal cheeses are deeper, and, as a result, one eats less of them. Give me a sliver of triple-cream raw–cow's milk cheese from a master cheese maker over a brick of low-fat flavorless dairy product from the assembly lines any day. When cooking, one needs far less Parmigiano-Reggiano to impact the flavor of a dish than a mountain of grated cardboard in the shelf-stable tins of a supermarket. Less really is more, especially when it comes to great cheese. Taking all of this into consideration, cheese and meat can be something as typical as the perfect cheeseburger (I like a thick slab of Hook's ten-year Cheddar from Wisconsin on mine!) or as novel as dressing up a humble shepherd's pie with Black Eagle Roquefort. Simple roasted chicken on Sunday evening can always use a new face, and certain cheeses, like Gruyère de Comté, are just the cheese to give it one. I encourage you to think outside the box and experiment with variations on your favorite barbecue/grill standards with an eye to how different cheeses might make them just a little bit better.

WINE NOTE

With meat, you can either pair *with* or *against* textures and flavors. You can take a big, fat steak and put a big, fat Cabernet with it—which is by and large the norm—or eat by more European standards and take a big, fat steak and put a higher-tone Burgundy, Barolo, or Rioja with it. These higher-toned wines cut into the meat, the acids peel the fat off your tongue, leaving the palette clean for the next wonderful bite. This is wine complementing food at its best.

Fowl and pork contain less fat than red meats, and therefore cannot tolerate a lot of tannin. However, the addition of cheese to pork and fowl dishes opens up a whole new level of wine-pairing possibilities. A wine that was once too big (with too much tannin or acidity) now comes into play. The fat in cheese tames the acid and tannin in bigger wines, so the flavors of the pork or poultry are allowed to come through rather than being overpowered by of the boldness of the wine.

Bite-size balls of delicately seasoned beef and pork, filled with the diminutive mozzarella balls known as *bocconcini* are braised in a super-simple tomato sauce. These meatballs are reminiscent of the famous Roman street food, *suppli al telefono* (so-called because of the resemblance the stretchy melted mozzarella bears to telephone wires). I enjoy letting guests discover the surprise inside what they thought were classic meatballs. If bocconcini are unavailable, fresh mozzarella balls can effectively be cut into 1-in/2.5-cm squares.

TO PREPARE THE MEATBALLS: Quickly submerge the bread slices in enough cold water to thoroughly soak them, then squeeze dry. Tear the hydrated bread into small pieces and place in a large mixing bowl. Add the basil, beef, pork, pecorino, eggs, salt, and a few grindings of pepper. Mix together with clean hands.

Form the mixture into twenty small patties, 2 in/5 cm in diameter. Lay a single bocconcini ball on each patty and then mold the meat mixture around the cheese to form meatballs. The meatballs can be prepared to this point up to a day ahead.

cont'd

TOMATO-BRAISED MEATBALLS WITH MELTING MOZZARELLA

SERVES 6 TO 8

FOR THE MEATBALLS
8 oz/225 g stale baguette or ciabatta bread, sliced

½ cup/30 g fresh basil, chopped

1 lb/455 g ground/minced beef

1 lb/455 g ground/minced pork

1 cup/100 g grated Pecorino Romano cheese

2 eggs, beaten

1 tsp salt

Freshly cracked black pepper

20 bocconcini di mozzarella cheese

TO PREPARE THE SAUCE: Heat the olive oil in a large saucepan over low heat. Add the onions and cook for about 10 minutes, or until translucent. Add the garlic, turn up the heat to medium, and cook for 3 to 4 minutes, or until the garlic is gilded and aromatic. Add the tomatoes, season well with salt and pepper, and add the chilies.

Simmer the sauce for 20 minutes, stirring often. Remove from the heat and allow to cool completely. Puree the sauce in a food mill or food processor fitted with the blade attachment.

TO ASSEMBLE THE DISH: In a deep saucepan large enough to hold the meatballs and sauce, heat the olive oil until hot but not smoking. Brown the meatballs, a few at a time, turning them from time to time to sear all around. Be careful not to crowd the pan, which will reduce the temperature and prevent a good searing. Transfer browned meatballs as they are finished to a large plate and continue until all of the meatballs are browned. Drain some of the oil and cooking fats from the pan, leaving some behind. Deglaze the bottom of the pan with the water, scraping the bottom of the pan with a wooden spoon to get all the delicious bits. Add the pureed tomato sauce and then the meatballs, gently pressing them into the sauce. Bring to a simmer and gently cook for 10 minutes.

Remove the meatballs from the heat and serve hot with plenty of sauce alongside.

RED WINE: Salice Salentino, Chianti Classico, Aglianico

FOR THE SAUCE
6 tbsp/90 ml extra-virgin olive oil

2 small onions, minced

3 garlic cloves, peeled

2 lb/910 g fresh or canned San Marzano or plum tomatoes, peeled, seeded, and chopped

Salt and freshly cracked black pepper

Pinch of crushed red chilies

FOR ASSEMBLING THE DISH
¼ cup/60 ml extra-virgin olive oil

½ cup/120 ml water

SAUSAGES STUFFED WITH TRUFFLE CHEESE

MAKES 6 SAUSAGES

6 sweet Italian sausages (approx. 1½ lb/680 g)

3 oz/85 g Caciotta al Tartufo or other truffle cheese, shredded

Crusty loaf of bread, for serving

The best butchers in Italy come from the sleepy Umbrian village of Norcia. This is less of an opinion and more of a well-known fact, so much so that butcher shops all over Italy are often called *Norcineria*, referring to a time when these famous masters of butchery would travel to other regions of Italy selling their skills. In addition to the renowned pecorinos and caciotta of the area, the medieval village of Norcia is also famous for its black truffles, and a festival is held in late February to celebrate the mighty *Tuber melanosporum*.

So, the combination of sweet pork sausages and truffle cheese was inevitable. Caciotta al Tartufo is a heavenly blend of buttery cow's milk and tangy sheep's milk studded with black truffles from Norcia. It is a delicious table cheese, with a unique texture making it the ultimate choice for this recipe. Tuscany's Boschetto al Tartufo or the milder Sottocenere would work nicely as well.

Since the possibilities are endless with this concept, I encourage you to use your imagination when cooking with cheese and sausage: duck sausages with goat cheese, chicken apple sausages with Cheddar, and on and on.

Preheat the oven to 400°F/200°C/gas 6.

Lay the sausages out on a baking sheet/tray. Roast for 20 minutes, or until the internal temperature on a thermometer reads 150°F/65°C. Remove from the oven and let cool completely.

Create a pocket in each sausage by cutting a slit that goes halfway through down the middle two-thirds of the length. Using your fingers, carefully pry open the pocket, being careful not to open it too wide, and stuff some of the shredded cheese inside. Distribute the cheese evenly among the sausages.

Heat a gas grill/barbecue to medium-high heat or build a medium-hot fire in a wood/charcoal grill/barbecue. Cook the sausages cheese-side up, for 10 to 12 minutes, or until the sausages are crispy and the cheese is melted. These sausages can also be prepared on the stove in a large sauté pan or flat-top griddle; cook the sausages over medium-high heat until they are crispy and the cheese is melted.

Serve hot with a good crusty loaf of bread.

WHITE WINE: Soave, Orvieto
RED WINE: Lambrusco, Bugey

SHEPHERD'S PIE WITH ROQUEFORT MASH

SERVES 4 TO 6

FOR THE MASH

2.2 lb/1 kg Yukon gold potatoes

⅔ cup/165 ml whole milk

4 tbsp/55 g butter, at room temperature

4 oz/115 g Roquefort cheese

Salt

FOR THE PIE

3 tbsp extra-virgin olive oil

2 small yellow onions, chopped

2.2 lb/1 kg leftover roast lamb, coarsely chopped, plus any roasting juices left over from lamb

1 cup/240 ml red wine

2 tbsp ketchup/tomato sauce

2 tbsp Worcestershire sauce

Salt and freshly cracked black pepper

I often wonder if shepherd's pie is a delicious, heart-warming way to use leftover roasted leg of lamb, or whether roasting a leg of lamb is subconsciously done for the excuse to make shepherd's pie. Either way, the addition of Roquefort,* a raw–sheep's milk blue, is in keeping with the shepherd theme of this classic and adds a wonderful richness to the potatoes.

The best-quality Roquefort may seem a bit cost prohibitive for such humble pub grub, but I can assure you that for the small amount of cheese required, it is worth getting the best. My particular favorite is *L'Aigle Noir* (The Black Eagle) made by ninety-six-year-old Jacques Carles, who still uses rounds of local rye bread to create the mold. Enter Chantal Plasse, an amazing *affinuer*, or cheese ager, who picks the top wheels from Monsieur Carles and ages them to perfection before labeling them The Black Eagle. Intense, creamy, and crumbly, the experience of this cheese lingers, so much so that ten minutes after tasting, one is still discovering new flavors that haunt the palate.

*Please indulge me in the telling of the story behind Roquefort: A young shepherd in Roquefort-suz-Souzon, France, sat down at the mouth of a cave to eat his lunch of rye bread, sheep's milk cheese, and, most likely, a glass of wine. His attention was drawn to a beautiful girl wandering the fields. Being French, his desire for hunger gave way to a much stronger desire, and he quickly left his meal at the mouth of the cave. The unique alchemical elements in the cave went to work on the mold that began to grow on the bread next to the fresh sheep's milk cheese. Several months later, after losing the girl, the shepherd returned to find the world's first piece of Roquefort.

TO PREPARE THE MASH: Peel the potatoes and cut into 1-in/ 2.5-cm cubes. Add to a pot of well-salted cold water and bring to a boil. Cook the potatoes until tender, about 20 minutes, and then drain. Meanwhile, gently heat the milk to a simmer and then remove from the heat. Using a food mill, ricer, or masher, mash the potatoes until smooth. Add the hot milk and butter along the way. Crumble the Roquefort over the potatoes and mix well. Season with salt and set aside.

TO PREPARE THE PIE: In a saucepan large enough to hold all of the ingredients, heat the olive oil over medium heat. Add the onions and cook, for about 20 minutes, or until they are translucent and slightly gilded. Increase the heat to medium-high and add the lamb. Sauté with the onions for 3 to 4 minutes, or until just beginning to turn golden. At this point, add any leftover roasting juices from the lamb, along with the wine, ketchup/tomato sauce, and Worcestershire sauce. Season with salt and pepper. (But do remember that the Roquefort in the mash will add quite a bit of salt to the overall dish.) Reduce the heat and gently simmer for 10 minutes, adding a splash of wine, water, or stock if too dry.

Preheat the oven to 400°F/200°C/gas 6.

Pour the lamb into an 8-by-12-in/20-by-30.5-cm ceramic baking dish (or individual ramekins) and pile the Roquefort mash on top, covering the meat completely. Use a fork to whip up the surface of the mash, creating waves and peaks. Bake for 30 to 40 minutes, or until the mash is nicely browned on top and the sauce is bubbling up around the edges. Serve hot.

RED WINE: Sagrantino, Bandol, Nero d'Avola

Roncal has been made in one of seven villages in the Valle de Roncal of the Spanish Pyrenees for more than 700 years! It is an aged cheese made from the raw milk of sheep that graze the mountains around Navarre. Buttery and fruity, it carries a distinctive olive flavor and is far less salty than its more famous cousin Manchego.

Place the chops between two pieces of plastic wrap/cling film and beat with a meat tenderizer; flatten to ⅛ in/3 mm thick. Combine the bread crumbs, Roncal, mint, and a few grindings of pepper in a bowl. Beat the eggs in a separate bowl. Dip the lamb chops into the beaten eggs and then into the bread crumb mixture.

      Heat the oil in a large frying pan over medium heat until it is hot but not smoking. Lay the breaded lamb chops in the hot oil and cook for about 3 minutes on each side, until crispy and golden outside, but still nice and pink inside. Serve with wedges of lemon and a handful of fresh arugula/rocket, if desired.

RED WINE: Priorat, Bandol, Chianti Classico, and even Amarone

BREADED LAMB CHOPS WITH RONCAL AND FRESH MINT

SERVES 2

8 baby lamb chops, trimmed, with bone intact

1½ cups/170 g bread crumbs

¼ cup/25 g grated Roncal cheese

1 tbsp fresh mint, chopped

Freshly cracked black pepper

2 eggs

¼ cup/60 ml extra-virgin olive oil

Lemon wedges, for serving

Fresh arugula/rocket, for serving (optional)

The best Goudas are considered to be the Boeren-kaas, or farmhouse Gouda. They are a family of artisan, farm-made cheeses that, by law, are made from the raw milk of cows that are allowed to pasture from early April through late November. The cows' diet is varied and allows for the complex-flavored cheese. These cheeses are certainly worth seeking out.

Next, and quite splendid, are the Fabriekskaas, made from excellent-quality pasteurized milk and aged in historic warehouses by master cheese makers. Reypenaer is perhaps the best of these, and eating it is a religious experience, I can assure you. It is far creamier in texture than the larger production Gouda with very complex flavors that linger on and on.

More readily available are the larger production Gouda, of which there are some top-rung examples, not the least of which is Beemster. The eighteen-month Beemster Gouda is sharp and sweet in one, with wonderful crystals and a fantastic melting quality that lends itself perfectly to cooking.

While all of the above-mentioned Gouda are great cheeses for making an excellent macaroni and cheese, I find the complex sweet and sharp flavors of an aged Gouda are a perfect match for these juicy pork loin skewers.

cont'd

PORK LOIN SKEWERS WITH AGED GOUDA AND APRICOT MUSTARD

MAKES 12 SKEWERS

¼ tsp fennel seeds

½ cup/120 ml grainy mustard

½ cup/170 g apricot jam

2 lb/910 g boneless pork loin

9 oz/255 g aged Gouda cheese, shredded

6 tbsp/90 ml extra-virgin olive oil

Sea salt and freshly cracked black pepper

Using a mortar and pestle or spice grinder, crush the fennel seeds to a powder. Mix the crushed fennel with the mustard and jam in a small bowl. Slice the pork loin into twelve 2 oz/55 g steaks. Place each steak between two sheets of plastic wrap/cling film and pound with a meat tenderizer into ⅛-in-/3-mm-thick pieces.

Spread the apricot mustard on one side of each pork loin piece. Divide the cheese over the mustard. Roll the pork loin lengthwise in a jelly-roll fashion. Use metal or bamboo skewers to skewer the pork loin rolls lengthwise. Rub the pork loin with the olive oil and season well with salt and pepper.

Heat a flat-top griddle or large sauté pan over medium-high heat and cook the pork loin skewers for 3 to 4 minutes on each side, or until the cheese is melted and the pork is cooked through and deep golden brown.

Serve piping hot.

. . . .

WHITE WINE: Grüner Veltliner
RED WINE: Amarone, Châteauneuf-du-Pape

Rogue River Blue is by far the best American blue cheese ever made, in my very humble opinion. It somehow has every element that I look for in blue cheese. Deeply rich raw cow's milk, earthy blue veins, and a clean crisp finish from the grape leaves dipped in Clear Creek Pear Brandy that the wheels are wrapped in before being aged. Inspired by the great blue cheese traditions of Europe, the brilliant artisans who created this masterpiece make small batches, so that when the cheese is gone, we have to wait patiently for its return, allowing those other glorious blues of the world a chance to be rediscovered.

Heat a gas grill/barbecue to medium-high heat or build a medium-hot fire in a charcoal grill/barbecue. Season the steaks with salt and pepper at the last second before placing on the grill. Cook for 4 to 6 minutes per side. Turn the steak in 45-degree angles if you want cross-hatch marks.

    To see if your steak is done, you can cheat by inserting a meat thermometer into the center (cutting to peek inside loses too many precious juices for my money). A rare steak is around 110°F/42°C, medium-rare is around 120°F/48°C, medium is around 140°F/60°C, and well-done is just a waste of a perfectly wonderful steak. (Sorry.)

    Place 1 oz/30 g of cheese on each steak just as it comes off the grill/barbecue, close your eyes, and enjoy the single best steak you'll ever have.

RED WINE: from Pinot Noir and Barolo to Cabernet Sauvignon and Brunello

GRILLED RIB-EYE STEAKS WITH ROGUE RIVER BLUE

SERVES 2

2 grass-fed organic beef rib-eye steaks, 7 to 8 oz/200 to 225 g each

Coarse sea salt and freshly ground black pepper

2 oz/60 g Rogue River Blue cheese, at room temperature

ROASTED QUAIL WITH BREAD AND ROCCOLO CHEESE SAUCE

SERVES 4

FOR THE SAUCE

2 cups/480 ml whole milk

½ yellow onion, peeled and studded with 3 cloves

Salt

1 cup/115 g best-quality bread crumbs

8 oz/225 g Roccolo cheese, grated

⅓ cup/75 ml heavy/double cream

Freshly cracked black pepper

Fresh nutmeg

Pinch of cayenne pepper

There is an old Italian proverb threatening that every crumb of bread dropped in this life will have to be picked up in purgatory using one's eyelashes! I need no such motivation for saving leftover bread, as its uses in the kitchen are countless and often priceless.

I love bread sauce. This is especially true since my friend Jerry Maybrook started making the most amazing sourdough in Los Angeles, providing my family with more fresh loaves per week than we can eat. I save the loaves in paper bags until they're rock hard and then shred them into nutty, delicious bread crumbs. They're great for using in meatballs, for frying in olive oil as a topping for light pastas and vegetable dishes, and for making this wonderful accompaniment to roasted birds.

Roccolo is a fantastically floral and rich raw-cow's milk cheese from Valtaleggio, Italy, that I happen to love crumbled over hot polenta served with game birds. You could substitute a combination of half Parmigiano-Reggiano and half Gruyère if Roccolo is unavailable.

TO PREPARE THE SAUCE: In a small saucepan over medium heat, slowly bring the milk to a simmer with the onion and a pinch of salt. Remove from the heat, let the onion infuse the milk for 5 minutes, and then discard the onion. Whisk the bread crumbs and cheese into the warm milk and return the mixture to the stove over a low heat, stirring constantly for 10 to 15 minutes, until the sauce has thickened.

Add the cream and season with salt, pepper, a few scrapes of fresh nutmeg, and the cayenne pepper. Transfer to a double boiler with a small piece of plastic wrap/cling film directly on top of the sauce to prevent a skin from forming.

TO PREPARE THE QUAIL: Preheat the oven to 450°F/230°C/gas 8.

Rinse the quail with cold water and pat dry. Place a sage leaf inside each cavity and then season all over with salt and pepper. Wrap a slice of pancetta around each quail. Heat the olive oil in a large ovenproof sauté pan over medium-high heat until hot but not smoking. Sear the quail, breast-side down, for 1 to 2 minutes, or until deep golden brown. Transfer the sauté pan to the oven and roast the quail (still breast-side down) for 4 to 5 minutes, or until cooked through but still juicy. Turn the quail over and return the pan to the oven for 1 minute longer.

Serve two quail per person atop a generous ladle of the bread and cheese sauce.

. . . .

WHITE WINE: Greco di Tufo
RED WINE: Burgundy, Barolo

FOR THE QUAIL
8 semi-boneless quail

8 fresh sage leaves

Salt and freshly cracked black pepper

8 paper-thin slices pancetta

2 tbsp extra-virgin olive oil

POUSSIN WITH GRUYÈRE DE COMTÉ

SERVES 2 TO 4

2 poussin or game hens

Salt and freshly cracked black pepper

4 tbsp/60 g unsalted butter

2 tbsp extra-virgin olive oil

2 garlic cloves, peeled

1½ cups/360 ml dry white wine, preferably Jura

1 cup/240 ml chicken stock

½ cup/60 g all-purpose/plain flour

8 oz/225 g Gruyère de Comté cheese, shredded

This is a simple, classic home-style dish from the Jura Mountains in the French Alps. A well-raised large farm hen is a more classic bird to use for this recipe, but I love the rich flavor and diminutive serving sizes of game hens or poussin.

Cut the poussin into quarters and season well with salt and pepper.

Heat the butter and olive oil in a large, heavy-bottomed sauté pan over medium-high heat. Add the poussin pieces and garlic. As soon as the garlic is deep golden brown, after about 7 minutes, remove and discard it. Continue browning the birds well on both sides, 3 to 4 minutes more. Transfer the browned poussin to a large plate and wipe the bottom of the pan with a few paper towels to get rid of any burnt butter residue and excess fat.

Add the wine and stock to the pan and bring to a boil. Reduce the heat to low and slip the poussin into the simmering liquid. Cover and continue to cook over a low flame for 10 to 15 minutes, or until the poussin are cooked through.

Preheat the oven to broil.

Transfer the cooked poussin, skin-side up, to an ovenproof serving dish or roasting pan. Bring the cooking liquid back to a boil and whisk in the flour and shredded cheese. Continue cooking for 2 to 3 minutes, or until a thick, smooth, and velvety sauce forms. Season with salt and pepper.

Drape the sauce over the poussin with a large kitchen spoon or ladle. Place the poussin under the broiler/grill for 3 to 5 minutes, or until the sauce is golden brown and bubbling.

Serve hot.

WHITE WINE: Chardonnay from Jura, Rioja Blanco
RED WINE: the lighter Garnachas of Spain, Châteauneuf-du-Pape

APPLE TART WITH LES DÉLICE DES CRÉMIERS, ALMONDS, AND HONEY / 203

GOAT CHEESE QUENELLES WITH STRAWBERRY
AND BALSAMIC VINEGAR COULIS / 207

COACH FARM TRIPLE-CREAM GOAT CHEESECAKE WITH LEMON CREAM / 208

EXTRA-VIRGIN OLIVE OIL CUPCAKES WITH
LEMONY MASCARPONE FROSTING / 210

CRÊPES WITH MASCARPONE AND HAZELNUT HONEY CREAM / 213

RICOTTA FRITTERS WITH CHOCOLATE / 215

SARDINIAN PECORINO FRITTERS WITH BLACKBERRY HONEY / 216

DESSERTS

Throughout European homes, cheese often *is* the dessert. Fresh or dried fruits, a handful of nuts, and a local cheese is a delicious and sensible way to end a meal. It encourages conversation, and, therefore, better digestion, as the cracking of walnuts from their shells and the chipping off chunks of aged cheeses become the focus of friends and family sharing the day's experience into the evening. Fresh figs, ripe strawberries, sweet peaches, and juicy cherries are delightul summertime fruits that can be served with creamy fresh goat cheeses Robiola from Piedmonte and Tomme de Ma Grande-mère from the Loire Valley. One particularly luscious pairing is a sliver of the silky triple-cream cow's milk from Paris, Brillat-Savarin (named after the master! gastronome, Jean Anthelme Brillat-Savarin) with summer's best strawberries and a glass of Champagne.

Sheep's milk Abbaye de Belloc made by Benedictine monks in the French Pyrenees or aged pecorinos from Northern Italy are great flavors to complete a meal with, perhaps drizzled with warm honey. And of course, the king of Italian aged cheeses, Parmigiano-Reggiano, makes for a regal and austere finish to a meal when dressed with a drop of aged, syrupy cooked grape must or artisinal balsamic vinegar and a pile of toasted hazelnuts.

Still, people all over the world are using cheese more and more in their pastries as well. Ice cream with Roquefort has become something of a novelty, as has chocolate brownies with goat cheese. I find that most modern households aren't accustomed to serving dinner in courses in the first place, so a cheese course and dessert course can be united to add a surprising finish to an elegant meal.

WINE NOTE

For me, dessert doesn't mean that the wine suddenly stops pouring. If I still have half a bottle of Barolo left on the table, that's what I'm drinking with dessert. You got a sweet tooth? Have yourself a glass of Port.

Personally, though, I prefer lighter-style dessert wine if I am going to partake at all. I gravitate toward the airiness of Moscato d'Asti, Prosecco, and the nonsparkling Chenin Blanc of the Loire, as well as Vin Santo, Sercial Madeira, and Rivesaltes Ambré that move more in the direction of Port. Red or white, sweet or dry—there are many heavenly pairings that can end the meal: think fresh berries and dry Champagne, for example, or chocolate-anything and Bugey, or panna cotta and Moscato d'Asti.

Here are some of my favorite pairings of classic desserts and wines:
- Apple tart and Sercial Madeira
- Bread pudding and Rivesaultes Ambré
- Fig tart and Trockenbeerenauslese (sweet German Riesling)
- Simple cakes, cookies, or donuts and Prosecco
- Sticky toffee pudding and Pedro Ximénez Sherry

Not exactly the old diner special of apple pie and Cheddar, this is a recipe for an apple and cheese dessert taken to the limits and beyond.

Les Délice des Crémiers is a triple-cream cow's milk cheese from Burgundy made of cream, double cream, and crème fraîche. The cheese has nutty flavors and a silky, velvety paste that goes naturally with apples or grapes. St. André, Pierre Robert, Explorateur, and Brillat-Savarin are lovely triple-cream cow's milk cheese that would also work well.

TO PREPARE THE DOUGH: Cut the butter into small cubes and place in a medium mixing bowl with the flour. Rub the butter into the flour with your hands until a coarse meal is formed.

Transfer the mixture to the bowl of a food processor fitted with the blade attachment. Add the crème fraîche and pulse just until a dough forms. Stop the machine immediately.

Take the dough in your hands and slam it down onto a very lightly floured work surface. Gather up the dough and continue to slam it down hard, a good ten to twelve times more. (This will help prevent the dough from rising too much during baking.) Wrap the dough in plastic wrap/cling film and chill for at least 1 hour.

Preheat the oven to 400°F/200°C/gas 6.

cont'd

APPLE TART WITH LES DÉLICE DES CRÉMIERS, ALMONDS, AND HONEY

MAKES ONE 15-IN/38-CM TART

FOR THE DOUGH

7 tbsp/100 g unsalted butter, chilled

3 cups/380 g all-purpose/plain flour

¼ cup/60 ml crème fraîche

FOR THE TART

3 tart green apples

3 tbsp unsalted butter

2 tbsp wildflower honey

8 oz/225 g Les Délice des Crémiers or similar triple-cream cow's milk cheese

¼ cup/30 g slivered almonds

TO ASSEMBLE THE TART: Peel and core the apples. Cut them into ⅛-in-/3-mm-thick slices. Heat 2 tbsp of the butter with the honey in a frying pan over low heat. Add the apple slices and sauté for 2 to 3 minutes, or until slightly gilded but still quite firm. Remove from the heat and allow to cool.

Turn the wheel of cheese on its side and cut it into discs as thin as possible. Roll out the pastry dough to a 15-in/ 38-cm circle. Place the dough circle on a baking sheet/tray (I like a pizza pan for this) and prick it all over with a fork. Arrange the apple slices in a concentric circle, leaving about a ½-in/12-mm border. Roll up the edges of the tart and pinch to form a simple crust. Scatter the slices of cheese and the almonds across the top of the apples. Dot with the remaining butter and bake for 15 minutes, or until the dough is cooked on the bottom and the cheese is melted and bubbly. Serve hot or at room temperature.

. . . .

WINE: Sercial Madeira

This is a delightful end to an elegant summer evening meal, when heavy desserts won't do and you have probably been eating ice cream all day to stay cool! Seek out the very best-quality chèvre like Petit Billy, Cypress Grove Chevre, or a very fresh goat cheese from a local artisan if you are fortunate enough to find one! Raspberries or blueberries are also a nice variation, depending on what is in season.

In a medium bowl, whisk together the goat cheese and cream until smooth, light, and airy. Cover with plastic wrap/cling film and chill for 30 minutes.

Meanwhile, place the strawberries in the bowl of a food processor fitted with the blade attachment. Puree the strawberries until smooth. Add the vinegar and sugar. Strain through a mesh sieve and chill.

When ready to serve, form the goat cheese–cream mixture into six quenelles using two large soupspoons. Pool the strawberry puree onto six individual plates and then transfer a single quenelle to the center of each plate.

Garnish with the fresh mint and serve with the shortbread.

WINE: Bugey, Lambrusco

GOAT CHEESE QUENELLES WITH STRAWBERRY AND BALSAMIC VINEGAR COULIS

SERVES 6

7 oz/200 g best-quality fresh goat cheese

¼ cup/60 ml heavy/double cream

12 very ripe strawberries, washed and stemmed

1 tbsp best-quality balsamic vinegar

3 tbsp sugar (depending on sweetness of fruit)

6 mint sprigs, for garnish

Shortbread, for serving

COACH FARM TRIPLE-CREAM GOAT CHEESECAKE WITH LEMON CREAM

MAKES ONE 10-IN/25-CM CHEESECAKE

FOR THE CRUST

1½ cups/150 g finely crushed oat biscuits (I use Hob Nobs)

5 tbsp/70 g unsalted butter, melted

Inspired by the master cheese makers of France, Miles and Lillian Cahn retired from the massive success of their Coach, Inc., leather company to live a calmer life making cheese in upstate New York. In a very short time, Coach Farm Dairy in Hudson Valley became one of the top artisanal cheese makers in the world. Their award-winning Triple Cream Goat cheese is unbelievable with fresh strawberries and is the feature of this unusual take on another New York classic, cheesecake. Triple-cream cheese can often have a bitter bite at the end, but this cheese is pure sweet cream and butter.

The crust is made from British oat biscuits instead of graham crackers, adding sweetness to the crust and a delightful contrast to the deep, creamy goat flavor of the cheese. A sliver of this goes a long way and is wonderful alone or with a dollop of Lemon Cream. The cheesecake lasts for several days and is actually better if served the day after making.

TO PREPARE THE CRUST: Preheat the oven to 350°F/180°C/ gas 4.

Use a 10-in/25-cm nonstick springform pan or butter the bottom and sides of a regular 10-in/25-cm springform pan. Place the crushed biscuits into a medium bowl and mix well with the melted butter. Press the biscuit crumbs firmly onto the bottom of the prepared pan. Bake the crust until it is firm and beginning to darken, 10 to 12 minutes. Remove and let cool.

TO PREPARE THE CHEESECAKE: Trim the goat cheese of any rind, taking care not to waste any of the interior cheese. Place the cheese in the bowl of an electric mixer fitted with the paddle attachment and cream with the sugar until smooth. Beat in the butter. Add the cream in a steady stream. Turn the machine to low and add the eggs, one at a time, allowing each egg to incorporate before adding the next. Add the vanilla and turn off the machine. The batter may appear to have broken a bit, but that is perfectly fine. Pour the batter onto the crust and spread evenly. Place the springform pan in a large roasting pan and add enough hot water to come halfway up the sides of the springform pan.

Bake the cheesecake for 45 minutes. Do not open the oven door during baking. Turn off the heat and allow the cheesecake to cool in the oven for 1 hour without opening the oven door.

Remove the cheesecake and let cool, uncovered, in the refrigerator overnight. This is a cake that *must* be allowed to set for the flavors to mellow and mingle.

TO PREPARE THE CREAM: In a large bowl, whip together the cream and zest with a whisk until soft peaks form.

When ready to serve, run the tip of a knife around the pan sides to loosen the cheesecake before unsnapping the springform sides. Cut into thin slices and serve cold or at room temperature with lemon cream.

WINE: Coteaux du Layon, Prosecco

FOR THE CHEESECAKE

1½ lb/680 g Coach Farm Triple Cream Goat cheese or fresh chèvre

1 cup/200 g light brown sugar

2 tbsp unsalted butter, melted and cooled

½ cup/120 ml heavy/double cream

3 eggs

1 tsp vanilla extract

FOR THE LEMON CREAM

2 cups/480 ml heavy/double cream

Zest of 2 lemons

EXTRA-VIRGIN OLIVE OIL CUPCAKES WITH LEMONY MASCARPONE FROSTING

MAKES 12 CUPCAKES

FOR THE CUPCAKES
2 cups/255 g all-purpose/plain flour

1½ tsp baking powder

Pinch of salt

1 cup/200 g granulated sugar

Zest of 2 lemons

⅔ cup/165 ml best-quality fruity extra-virgin olive oil

3 eggs

½ cup/120 ml freshly squeezed lemon juice

Airy and light, these little olive oil cakes are frosted with silky smooth mascarpone cheese folded into whipped cream scented with lemon.

I remember having these at the Slow Food Nation conference in San Francisco, where 80,000 people descended upon the City by the Bay to see firsthand what amazing artisanal products were being crafted by people all around the country. It was a glorious week, a promise of things moving toward a better attitude about the foods we eat and the environment they come from.

TO PREPARE THE CUPCAKES: Preheat the oven to 350°F/180°C/gas 4. Place paper liners in twelve cups of a muffin pan/tin.

In a medium bowl, sift together the flour, baking powder, and salt.

In a large bowl, combine the granulated sugar and lemon zest. Add the olive oil and mix well. Add the eggs, one at a time, mixing well after each addition. Add the dry ingredients in three additions alternating with the lemon juice in two additions, beginning and ending with the dry ingredients. Mix the batter until combined.

Fill the cupcake liners about three-quarters of the way full with the batter. Place the pan in the oven and bake for about 20 minutes, or until a wooden skewer inserted into the center comes out clean. Remove from the oven and let cool completely.

TO PREPARE THE FROSTING: In the bowl of an electric mixer fitted with the whisk attachment, whip the cream until stiff peaks form. In a separate bowl, whisk together the mascarpone, powdered/icing sugar, and lemon zest until smooth. Gently fold the whipped cream into the mascarpone mixture.

Using a spatula, frost the cooled cupcakes and decorate with candied violet petals, if desired. The cupcakes can be served the same day or kept unfrosted in an airtight container at room temperature for up to 3 days.

. . . .

WINE: Vin Santo, finer Marsala

FOR THE FROSTING

1 cup/240 ml heavy/double cream

8 oz/225 g mascarpone cheese, at room temperature

½ cup/60 g powdered/icing sugar, sifted

Zest of 1 lemon

12 candied violet petals (optional)

I had always made these crêpes with a citrus or honeysuckle honey, until I discovered the culinary "crack" of Floriano Turco. The ex-insurance salesman from the northern Italian city of Cuneo blends fresh roasted hazelnuts from Piedmonte into a hand-harvested wildflower honey. Imagine caramel, hazelnut butter, and floral honey in one bite together with the tang and texture of mascarpone.

The result, known as Floriano Hazelnut Cream, is available online, as well as from some specialty food shops and cheesemongers. It is not inexpensive, but a little goes a long way and this is one of those rare treats worth splurging for if you can.

In a medium bowl, whisk together the eggs, olive oil, milk, and flour to form a smooth batter. Cover and let rest for at least 1 hour, though 2 to 3 hours is best. The batter should coat the back of a spoon nicely. If it's too thick, add a splash more milk.

Heat a 10-in-/25-cm-diameter nonstick frying pan over medium heat. Wipe the pan with a paper towel greased with a small amount of the butter. Pour enough batter to thinly cover the bottom of the pan, about ¼ cup/60 ml. Cook for 2 to 3 minutes, or until golden brown on one side. Carefully loosen and lift the edges with a metal spatula. Flip the crêpe and cook for another minute. Transfer the crêpe to large plate and repeat with the remaining batter to make about 12 crêpes.

Preheat the oven to 225°F/110°C/gas ¼.

Divide the mascarpone among the crêpes, spreading it to the edges, and then fold the crêpes into quarters. Place the finished crêpes on a baking sheet/tray lined with parchment/baking paper and place them in the oven for 2 to 3 minutes, or until just warmed through. Gently warm the hazelnut cream by placing the closed jar in a warm water bath. Transfer the crêpes to individual plates, drizzle with warm hazelnut cream, and serve immediately.

WINE: Moscato d'Asti

CRÊPES WITH MASCARPONE AND HAZELNUT HONEY CREAM

MAKES 12 TO 14 CRÊPES

3 eggs

1½ tbsp extra-virgin olive oil

1½ cups/360 ml whole milk, plus more if needed

¾ cup/90 g all-purpose/plain flour

Butter, for greasing crêpe pan

12 oz/340 g mascarpone cheese

½ cup/120 ml Floriano Hazelnut Cream or citrus blossom honey

I experienced a version of this recipe on my very first trip to Rome many years ago at a little osteria behind Santa Maria in Trastevere, just south of Vatican City. Hot desserts are often the stuff of restaurants, as nobody really wants to get up and start cooking dessert after a meal at home, but the promise of warm creamy ricotta with bittersweet chocolate is worth a little push toward the kitchen.

In a medium bowl, mix together the ricotta, flour, chocolate, pine nuts, sugar, eggs, and orange zest. Using a scoop or large soupspoon, gather enough of the mixture to form a ball the size of a golf ball. Continue with the remaining ricotta mixture to make about 12 balls. (The recipe can be made up to this point a few hours before frying if the balls are kept refrigerated.)

Heat the grapeseed oil in a deep-sided frying pan to 350°F/180°C. Roll the balls of ricotta in flour, shaking off any excess. Slip a few balls at a time into the hot oil and cook for about 3 minutes, or until deep golden and hot throughout. Drain on paper towels, dust with powdered/icing sugar, and serve piping hot.

· ·

WINE: Although we haven't discussed specific wines by name, there is one perfect wine for this dish: Luli Vino Chinato is a Moscato from Piedmonte, which tastes like cinnamon-laced Sauternes. A Moscato from Asti or a Vin Santo from Tuscany would also be lovely.

RICOTTA FRITTERS WITH CHOCOLATE

MAKES 12 FRITTERS

12 oz/340 g fresh ricotta cheese, well drained

⅔ cup/80 g all-purpose/plain flour, plus extra for rolling

3 oz/85 g dark chocolate, chopped

¼ cup/30 g pine nuts, toasted

¼ cup/50 g sugar

2 eggs

Zest of 1 orange

1 cup/240 ml grapeseed or vegetable oil, for frying

Powdered/icing sugar, for dusting

Known as *sebadas* in Sardinia, these are basically fried ravioli filled with fresh pecorino, perfumed with orange zest, and doused with golden honey. The tang of fresh pecorino is a wonderful balance to the sweet honey, and a young Manchego or Pyrenees sheep's milk cheese would do nicely, if need be.

Try to find a jar of honey from Dr. Paolo Pescia, a passionate second-generation honey maker from Tuscany, who transports his beehives to seasonally flowering zones and national parks, a kind of "nomadic" beekeeper. This laborious process creates a series of monofloral honeys that are pure alchemy. I particularly love the blackberry honey for these pecorino fritters.

SARDINIAN PECORINO FRITTERS WITH BLACKBERRY HONEY

SERVES 4

1⅓ cups/220 g semolina

1⅓ cups/165 g all-purpose/plain flour

¼ tsp sea salt

4 eggs; 1 beaten for sealing dough

1 cup/240 ml water

2 tbsp extra-virgin olive oil

1 lb/455 g fresh pecorino cheese, shredded

1 orange, for zesting

2 cups/480 ml pure olive oil or grapeseed oil, for frying

Blackberry or other wildflower honey, for drizzling

In a large bowl, whisk together the semolina, all-purpose/plain flour, and salt. Make a well in the center. Add 3 eggs, the water, and the extra-virgin olive oil into the well and beat with a fork, slowly incorporating the flour until a sticky dough begins to form.

Turn out the mixture onto a well-floured work surface and knead for 5 minutes, or until the dough is smooth and shiny. Wrap the dough in plastic wrap/cling film and chill for at least 30 minutes.

Roll out the dough to a thickness of 1/16 in/2 mm. Using a fluted pasta cutter or sharp knife, cut circles 4 in/10 cm in diameter. Brush the circles of dough with the remaining beaten egg and place a small mound of pecorino in the center. Finely grate the orange zest over the pecorino.

Place the remaining discs of dough over the filling and seal them closed by pressing down all around the edges.

Heat the olive oil in a large, low-sided sauté pan to 350°F/180 C°. Slip the filled discs into the hot oil and fry for 2 to 3 minutes, flipping the discs over now and again to ensure even cooking. When the fritters are a nice golden brown, drain on paper bags or paper towels and serve immediately with plenty of honey.

WINE: Prosecco, Moscato d'Asti, Bugey

INDEX

NTINA CASTELMAGNO CACIOCAVALLO TALEGGIO MONTE ENEBRO HUMBOLE
NO-REGGIANO CHÈVRE NOIR MANOURI GOUDA FETA PROVOLONE STRACCHIN
OMAGER D'AFFINOIS MUNSTER MASCARPONE SBRINZ ROQUEFORT RONCA
BRIE CAMEMBERT ROBIOLA BOCCONCINI BURRATA FONTINA CASTELMAGN
RUFFLE TREMOR FROMAGE BLANC CHEDDAR PARMIGIANO-REGGIANO CHÈVR
OZZARELLA PETIT BASQUE PRIMO SALE BEAUFORT FROMAGER D'AFFINO
LICE DES CRÉMIERS GOAT TOMMINO GORGONZOLA BRIE CAMEMBERT ROB
NTE ENEBRO HUMBOLDT FOG RICOTTA PECORINO TRUFFLE TREMOR FROMA
PROVOLONE STRACCHINO CASCIOTTA D'URBINO MOZZARELLA PETIT BASQU
ROQUEFORT RONCAL ROCCOLO GRUYÈRE LES DÉLICE DES CRÉMIERS GO
TINA CASTELMAGNO CACIOCAVALLO TALEGGIO MONTE ENEBRO HUMBOLE
NO-REGGIANO CHÈVRE NOIR MANOURI GOUDA FETA PROVOLONE STRACCHIN
OMAGER D'AFFINOIS MUNSTER MASCARPONE SBRINZ ROQUEFORT RONCA
BRIE CAMEMBERT ROBIOLA BOCCONCINI BURRATA FONTINA CASTELMAG
RUFFLE TREMOR FROMAGE BLANC CHEDDAR PARMIGIANO-REGGIANO CHÈ
OZZARELLA PETIT BASQUE PRIMO SALE BEAUFORT FROMAGER D'AFF
LICE DES CRÉMIERS GOAT TOMMINO GORGONZOLA BRIE CAMEMBER
NTE ENEBRO HUMBOLDT FOG RICOTTA PECORINO TRUFFLE TREMOR
PROVOLONE STRACCHINO CASCIOTTA D'URBINO MOZZARELLA PET

TOMMINO GORGONZOLA BRIE CAMEMBERT ROBIOLA BOCCONCINI BURRA
RICOTTA PECORINO TRUFFLE TREMOR FROMAGE BLANC CHEDDAR PARM
ASCIOTTA D'URBINO MOZZARELLA PETIT BASQUE PRIMO SALE BEAUFORT
CCOLO GRUYÈRE LES DÉLICE DES CRÉMIERS GOAT TOMMINO GORGONZO
ACIOCAVALLO TALEGGIO MONTE ENEBRO HUMBOLDT FOG RICOTTA PECORINO
OIR MANOURI GOUDA FETA PROVOLONE STRACCHINO CASCIOTTA D'URBINO
UNSTER MASCARPONE SBRINZ ROQUEFORT RONCAL ROCCOLO GRUYÈRE LES
LA BOCCONCINI BURRATA FONTINA CASTELMAGNO CACIOCAVALLO TALEGGIO
LANC CHEDDAR PARMIGIANO-REGGIANO CHÈVRE NOIR MANOURI GOUDA FE
RIMO SALE BEAUFORT FROMAGER D'AFFINOIS MUNSTER MASCARPONE SB
OMMINO GORGONZOLA BRIE CAMEMBERT ROBIOLA BOCCONCINI BURRATA
G RICOTTA PECORINO TRUFFLE TREMOR FROMAGE BLANC CHEDDAR PARM
ASCIOTTA D'URBINO MOZZARELLA PETIT BASQUE PRIMO SALE BEAUFORT
CCOLO GRUYÈRE LES DÉLICE DES CRÉMIERS GOAT TOMMINO GORGONZO
OCAVALLO TALEGGIO MONTE ENEBRO HUMBOLDT FOG RICOTTA PECORIN
OIR MANOURI GOUDA FETA PROVOLONE STRACCHINO CASCIOTTA D'URBIN
UN MASCARPONE SBRINZ ROQUEFORT RONCAL ROCCOLO GRUYÈRE LE
A CINI BURRATA FONTINA CASTELMAGNO CACIOCAVALLO TALEGGIO
DAR PARMIGIANO-REGGIANO CHÈVRE NOIR MANOURI GOUDA